SAINSBURY'S

SEASONAL SALADS

CAROL BOWEN

ACKNOWLEDGEMENTS

Series Editor: **Nicola Hill**
Editor: **Mary-Clare Jerram**
Copy Editor: **Wendy Lee**
Art Editor: **Lisa Tai**
Designer: **Sue Storey**
Production Controller: **Alyssum Ross**
Photographer: **Clive Streeter**
Home Economist: **Lyn Rutherford**
Stylists: **Sue Russell-Fell and Maria Kelly**
Jacket Photographer: **Vernon Morgan**
Jacket Home Economist: **Allyson Birch**
Jacket Stylist: **Lorrie Mack**

NOTES

1. Standard level spoon measurements are used in all recipes.
1 tablespoon = one 15 ml spoon
1 teaspoon = one 5ml spoon

2. Both metric and imperial measurements have been given in all recipes. Use one set of measurements only and not a mixture of both.

3. Ovens should be preheated to the specified temperature – if using a fan assisted oven, follow manufacturer's instructions for adjusting the temperature.

4. Eggs should be size 3 unless otherwise stated.

5. Pepper should be freshly ground black pepper unless otherwise stated.

6. Fresh herbs should be used unless otherwise stated. If unavailable use dried herbs as an alternative but halve the quantities stated.

7. All microwave information is based on a 650 watt oven. Follow manufacturer's instructions for an oven with a different wattage.

Published exclusively for
J Sainsbury plc
Stamford Street, London SE1 9LL
by Cathay Books
Michelin House
81 Fulham Road, London SW3 6RB

First published 1989

ISBN 0 86178 563 0

Produced by Mandarin Offset in Hong Kong
Printed and Bound in Hong Kong

Contents

Introduction

Imaginative and exciting salad recipes bring out the best in fresh vegetables and fruit and enhance their flavours and textures, tempting you to prepare them through winter, spring and autumn, as well as summer.

Salads are dishes for any season, any occasion and any time of day, despite the myth that they are summer fare. The days when many thought of them as 'rabbit' food, purely for mid-summer eating, are long over; today, more than ever before, we happily munch, crunch and savour the delights of salads from January to December.

It is hardly surprising that salads have found favour – they offer such versatility of ingredients, wealth of valuable nutrients, and abundance of food choices for the slimmer, gourmet and gourmand alike, and can also demonstrate an ability to fit the bill when a side dish, main meal, appetizer or between-course cleanser is required.

Whatever part of the meal a salad forms, mixing and matching flavours, textures and colours is all-important. Never make compromises on quality – fresh, unblemished produce is a must and careful and imaginative preparation and presentation will bring fruitful rewards. If in doubt about the choice of ingredients, then follow the seasons, for each month will bring its own bounty of fruit and vegetables and nature will, of course, ensure the virtue of variety (see pages 8-9).

When choosing a main course salad, ensure that it has a vital protein food as its anchor. This could be meat, fish, cheese, eggs, nuts or pulses. Balance with a good variety of salad leaves, cooked pasta, rice or other grains, interesting vegetables and fruits and an appropriate dressing. The nutritional value of the ingredients in side salads and green salad accompaniments is not so critical but imaginative combinations of textures, colours and flavours will tease the palate and please the eye.

Preparation and Serving

Any salad needs to be carefully prepared. All leaves, vegetables and fruits should be washed, trimmed then sliced, diced, or cut as liked; they may be left raw, blanched, par-cooked or cooked, according to the recipe or purpose for which they are intended. Unless a recipe states otherwise, most salads are best prepared on the day of eating, preferably just before serving. This ensures that the ingredients are crisp, bright, resilient and fresh and that vitamins and minerals – so sensitive to heat, light and age – are still intact and retain their maximum value. Many salad ingredients, if washed and dried carefully and stored in the refrigerator, will keep for up to 3 days.

Always wash and dry salad components carefully – any water left behind will dilute the dressing. Dry in a salad spinner, on kitchen paper or between tea towels. Use a roomy serving dish or salad bowl so that the dressing can be added and tossed at the table with ease. Choose from china, pottery, wood and glass bowls; remember that if wood is used it is porous and difficult to clean, and flavours will soak into it that will never quite be removed. To toss the salad choose a blunt pair of salad servers that will not bruise the leaves or use your hands – the best tools.

Tossing a salad is an art, but one that can be learnt easily. Simply pour over the prepared dressing, and toss the salad from top to bottom and side to side until every single item in the mixture gleams with a thin coating of the dressing – then serve at once.

Salad Dressings

The basis for most salad dressings is an appropriate oil and a good vinegar, although the choice is anything but easy. Every oil and vinegar has its own specific colour, culinary purpose and character. The guide below, listing the oils and vinegars used in this book, gives you some idea of the choice available and suggests flavours that complement each other.

Oils

Grapeseed oil A rich green oil made from the seeds of grapes. It is popular in salad dressings, and is used for making margarine. Sometimes it is flavoured with sprigs of herbs.

Olive oil The undisputed king of salad oils – a good one will have a greenish-yellow colour. Two types can be found: virgin olive oil which is not bleached or deodorized; and pure olive oil which is hot-pressed from pulp and kernels and then treated. Look out for olive oil flavoured with herbs such as fennel (lovely for fish) and rosemary (especially good with lamb).

Safflower oil Rich in polyunsaturated fatty acids, this oil is excellent for salad dressings and for those following special diets.

Sesame oil A rich amber oil made from sesame seeds, it makes a splendid salad dressing for

Spring onion tassels

Radish roses

Striped mushrooms

oriental-style salads and is perfect for cooking Chinese meals.

Sunflower oil A very pale yellow, tasteless and odourless oil that is especially versatile. A good all-round oil for cooking and using in dressings.

Walnut oil A nutty-flavoured oil which has a rich golden colour. It is a favourite for salad dressings, but is rarely used for cooking purposes. A hazelnut oil is also available and can be used in a similar way.

Vinegars

Balsamic vinegar A vinegar with a strong, distinctive flavour, it is expensive but excellent in salad dressings. Use a good quality wine vinegar if balsamic is unavailable.

Cider vinegar A dark golden-brown vinegar made from apple pulp. It is good for general cooking purposes, in oriental-style cooking (instead of rice vinegar) and for salad dressings.

Malt vinegar A rich caramel-coloured vinegar that is mainly used for pickling rather than for salad dressings.

Wine vinegar There are several types – red, white, rosé and sherry – and all can be used in salad dressings. Many are available flavoured with herbs: for example, dill, tarragon, rosemary, thyme, bay leaves and basil. Others flavoured with chilli pepper, lemons, garlic, green peppercorns, strawberries, raspberries and shallots can be bought.

SALAD GARNISHES

When time is not at a premium, and you're all out to impress, a salad can be garnished in many different ways to give it added appeal.

Celery curls Trim the celery then cut into even lengths. Using a sharp knife, make several cuts along the length of the celery almost to the end. Place in iced water and leave for about 1 hour to curl.

Cucumber or citrus fruit slices, twists, cones and butterflies Slice the cucumber or citrus fruit thinly. Produce notched slices or wheels by scoring the cucumber or fruit along its length with a special canelle knife. For twists make a small cut from the outer edge of the cucumber or fruit to the centre. Twist the ends in opposite directions to give a twisted shape. Alternatively twist the ends towards one another to make a cone. To create butterflies, cut the cucumber or fruit slices in half and, in turn, cut from the outside peel edge almost into the centre. Open out.

Fragrant herb bows and bundles Fragrant herbs, with or without flowers, can be tied together in bundles with chives to make an attractive garnish for a salad.

Gherkin fans Make lengthways cuts almost to the end of each gherkin from the 'flower' end. Spread out carefully to make a fan shape.

Pepper rings and bundles Simply slice a pepper horizontally to make paper-thin rings for garnishing. For a more elaborate effect, slice one ring horizontally from the pepper then cut the rest of the pepper into thin strips and push into the ring.

Radish rose and waterlily For the rose, trim the radish and, using a sharp-pointed knife, cut a row of petal shapes around it, near to the base but keeping it intact. Repeat with a second row of petal shapes above the first row. Continue to the top of the radish. Place in iced water for 1-2 hours to open out. For a waterlily, trim the radish and make 8 deep, even cuts from the tip end to the base, but don't cut through the base. Place in iced water for 1-2 hours to open out.

Spring onion tassels Trim the spring onion at both ends. Using a sharp knife, make several cuts along the length of the green part of the onion. Place in iced water and leave for about 1 hour to curl.

Striped mushrooms Using a sharp knife or special canelle knife, remove thin strips of the outer flesh at regular intervals around the cap to give a striped effect.

Tomato rose and waterlily To make a rose remove the skin from a firm tomato with a sharp knife in one continuous strip, about 1 cm (½ inch) wide. Curl the strip, keeping the flesh side inside, from the base end, to make a rosebud shape. For a waterlily, make zigzag cuts around the waist of a firm tomato, cutting into the centre. Separate the two halves and place small sprigs of parsley in the centres.

Vegetable rolls and knots Peel carrots, cucumber or mooli with a knife or peeler into thin strips, then roll and secure with a wooden cocktail stick. Tie a knot in the centre of thin vegetables such as spring onions.

MAKING BASIC MAYONNAISE

2 egg yolks or 1 egg
1 tablespoon white wine vinegar or lemon juice
½ teaspoon salt
pinch of freshly ground white pepper
½ teaspoon dry mustard powder
300 ml (½ pint) olive oil (at room temperature)

Place the egg yolk (or whole egg) in a bowl and whisk with a balloon whisk, electric blender or use a food processor on medium speed until smooth, pale and creamy. Add vinegar or lemon juice, salt, pepper and mustard powder, whisking to blend.

Add the olive oil, drop by drop to begin with, whisking constantly. When the mixture starts to thicken and emulsify, dribble in the oil in a steady stream, whisking steadily to incorporate. Gradually increase the flow of the oil as the dressing thickens further and becomes very creamy. Beat until the mixture is thick and will not fall off the whisk when raised above the bowl. If the mayonnaise becomes too thick then thin with a little extra lemon juice.

Add any flavourings: for example, chopped herbs, chopped watercress, curry paste or powder with a little chopped mango chutney, or tomato purée with chilli powder or paprika.

To store the mayonnaise, cover and chill in the refrigerator. Fresh mayonnaise will keep for about 3 days. Whisk well before using.

MAKES 300 ML (½ PINT)

Nutritional content per quantity: **Carbohydrate: 1 g** **Fat: 319 g** **Kilocalories: 2910**

Whisking the egg

Dribbling in the oil

Increasing the flow of oil

Cooking and removing cooked flesh from a crab

Weigh the crab first. Fill a large pan with water and add 175 g (6 oz) salt to every 2-2.5 litres (3½-4 pints) of water. Bring the water to boil. Place the crab in the boiling water, cover the pan and simmer, allowing 15 minutes for the first 500 g (1 lb) of crab and then 8 minutes for each extra 500 g (1 lb).

When cooked, remove the crab from the pan and leave to cool. Keep it moist by covering with a damp tea towel.

To remove the flesh, lay the cooked crab on its back then press down, push forward and prise up with the thumbs so that the whole body with the legs as well will come free from the carapace.

Press on the small mouth part so that it snaps away. Discard the stomach (it resembles a small crinkled bag, and is near the mouth) and gills or 'dead men's fingers'.

Separate the white meat from the dark meat and place in bowls.

Crack the claws with a small hammer and pull out the flesh. Break the remaining small legs and push out the flesh with a long thin metal skewer. The empty claws and legs can be used for making fish stock.

Clean the crab shell by scrubbing it under the cold water tap thoroughly. Plunge in boiling water for 5 minutes and then drain.

Prising the body free of the carapace

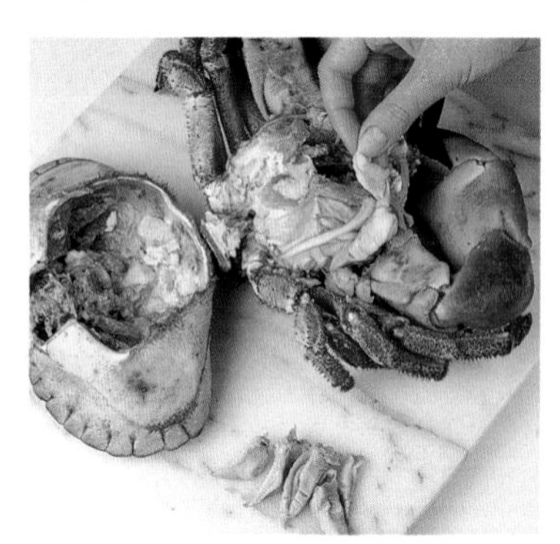

Removing the 'dead men's fingers'

Cracking the claws with a hammer

SEASONAL AVAILABILITY OF SALAD VEGETABLES AND FRUIT

The comprehensive chart below lists all the salad vegetables and fruits used in the recipes in this book, indicating when they are available in the shops, as home-grown or imported produce.

SALAD VEGETABLES

Leafy vegetables

Chicory Home-grown all year round. Imported all year round; *radicchio* imported October-May
Cress Home-grown all year round. Imported all year round
Endives *escarole* Imported October-May; *frisée* Home-grown and imported all year round
Lamb's lettuce Imported all year round
Lettuce *batavia* Imported October-May; *Cos* Home-grown April-November; *crisp* Home-grown April-November; *feuille de chêne* Home-grown and imported all year round; *iceberg* Home-grown and imported all year round; *round* Home-grown and imported all year round; *quattro stagione* Home-grown April-November
Spinach Home-grown in season May-July and September-November. *Forced spinach* available most of the year
Spring greens Home-grown April-May. Imported in summer
Watercress Home-grown March-November. Imported November-March

Tubers and roots

Beetroot Home-grown June-April. Imported April-June
Carrots Home-grown July-May. Imported all year round
Celeriac Available all year round
Horseradish Home-grown mainly available October-February. Imported all year round
Potatoes Home-grown *maincrop* September-July/August; *new potatoes* Home-grown May-September. Imported September-May
Mooli Home-grown autumn. Imported all year round
Radishes Home-grown April-October. Imported October-April

SEASONAL AVAILABILITY OF SALAD VEGETABLES AND FRUIT

Onion family

Garlic Available all year round. New-season garlic supply peaks in March and September
Leeks Generally available all year round. Home-grown summer leeks May-August and winter leeks November-March
Onions Home-grown July-May. Imported all year round
Spring onions Home-grown March-October. Imported November-February

Brassicas

Broccoli Home-grown *sprouting broccoli* available March-May and *calabrese* August-October. Imported all year round
Brussels sprouts Home-grown available September-April, supplemented with imported during this time too
Cabbage Home-grown *summer cabbages* August-September; *autumn* and *winter cabbages* October-February; *spring cabbage* April-May; and *red cabbage* September-May. All types imported all year round
Cauliflower Home-grown May-July. Imported all year round
Chinese leaves Home-grown May-December. Imported December-May
Spring greens Home-grown all year round

Pods and seeds

Beans *dwarf green* Home-grown July-October. Imported all year round; *green* Home-grown June-October. Imported all year round; *runner* Home-grown July-October. Imported all year round; *haricot* Home-grown June-October
Peas Home-grown June-August. Imported February-July
Sweetcorn Home-grown August-September. Imported all year round

Fruiting vegetables

Aubergine Home-grown July-October. Imported all year round
Avocado Imported all year round
Baby corn cobs Imported all year round
Courgettes Home-grown July-August. Imported all year round
Cucumber Home-grown March-October. Imported October-March
Peppers Home-grown June-October. Imported all year round
Tomatoes Home-grown April-October. All types, including *cherry tomatoes* and *extra large* imported all year round

Stems and shoots

Asparagus *White asparagus* May-June and *French asparagus* May-July
Bean sprouts All year round
Celery Home-grown available April-November. Imported available November-April
Sprouted alfalfa Home-grown all year round. Imported all year round
Fennel Home-grown August-September. Imported all year round

Mushrooms

Mushrooms All year round

Edible flowers

Nasturtium flowers and leaves Home-grown and imported during spring and summer months

FRUIT

Top fruit

Apples Home-grown August-April. Imported all year round
Cherries Home-grown June-July. Imported during the late spring and early summer
Nectarines Imported during the spring, summer and early autumn months
Peaches Imported almost all year round
Pears Home-grown October-April. Imported all year
Nuts Available all year round. New-season home-grown September-December

Soft fruit

Strawberries Home-grown mid May-September Imported all year round
Raspberries Home-grown June-September supplemented with imported fruit

Citrus fruit

Grapefruit Imported all year
Kumquats Imported December-July
Lemons Imported all year round
Limes Imported all year round
Oranges Imported all year round
Tangerines, satsumas, etc. Imported all year round

Exotic fruits

Bananas Imported all year round
Dates Imported all year round
Figs Home-grown and imported August-December
Grapes Imported all year round
Kiwi fruit Imported all year round
Lychees Imported December-February and June-August
Mangoes Imported all year round
Melon *cantaloupe* Imported all year round except winter; *charentais* Imported July-September; *galia* Imported all year round; *watermelon* Imported June-September
Paw-Paw Imported all year round
Pineapples Imported all year round
Pomegranates Imported September-January

SIMPLY GREEN SALADS

CRISP, LIGHT AND CRUNCHY, THESE SIMPLE GREEN SALAD IDEAS CAN BE ENJOYED AS MAIN COURSE ACCOMPANIMENTS, BETWEEN COURSE PALATE-CLEANSERS, OR WELCOME LIGHT STARTER DISHES. FOR ALL YEAR ROUND ECONOMY CHOOSE A RECIPE THAT REFLECTS THE BEST IN SEASON.

MINT, MELON AND CUCUMBER SALAD

THIS SIMPLE FRUITY GREEN SALAD CAN BE MADE WITH KIWI FRUIT INSTEAD OF MELON. ELECTRIC GREEN AND REFRESHINGLY SWEET YET PIQUANT, KIWI FRUIT MAKES THE PERFECT STAND-IN WHEN MELON IS NOT AT ITS BEST. PEEL AND SLICE IT THINLY TO SHOW OFF THE BRIGHT GREEN FLESH AND THE DECORATIVE VIOLET INNER RINGS

1 medium charentais or galia melon
½ cucumber
4-6 tablespoons Mint Dressing (see page 87)
2 tablespoons cashew nuts (optional)
mint sprigs to garnish

Halve the melon, then remove and discard the seeds. Using a melon baller or teaspoon, scoop out the flesh in small balls and place in a large bowl.

Peel the cucumber if liked, then cut into thin julienne strips and add to the melon with the dressing and cashew nuts, if used. Toss gently to coat and mix. Serve garnished with mint sprigs.

SERVES 4

Nutritional content per serving: Carbohydrate: 9 g Fat: 12 g Fibre: 2 g Kilocalories: 156

WINTER GREEN SALAD

GREEN SALADS WERE ORIGINALLY INTENDED AS PALATE-CLEANSERS BUT THEY HAVE COME A LONG WAY SINCE THEN. VARY THE GREEN LEAVES AND VEGETABLES IN THIS SALAD AS THE WINTER SEASON PROGRESSES AND DIFFERENT TYPES OF LETTUCE, NEW YOUNG SPINACH, WATERCRESS AND HERBS APPEAR

½ small white cabbage, cored and shredded finely
2 sticks celery, chopped
1 head chicory, separated into spears
1 green dessert apple, cored and chopped
about 50 g (2 oz) frisée or escarole, torn into pieces
1 bunch watercress
½ head fennel, sliced
¼ onion, sliced very thinly
handful of chopped mixed herbs (for example, chives, young sorrel, parsley and chervil)
DRESSING:
4 tablespoons walnut or hazelnut oil
1-2 tablespoons white wine vinegar or raspberry vinegar
salt and pepper

Place the cabbage, celery, chicory, apple, frisée, watercress, fennel, onion and herbs in a large salad bowl, tearing any large leaves into bite-sized pieces.

To make the dressing, beat the oil with the vinegar and salt and pepper to taste until well blended. Alternatively, place all the ingredients in a screw-top jar or bottle and shake vigorously to blend.

Pour over the salad just before serving and toss lightly to coat and mix. Serve at once.

SERVES 4-6

Nutritional content per serving: Carbohydrate: 10 g Fat: 15 g Fibre: 6 g Kilocalories: 196

Mint, Melon and Cucumber Salad; Winter Green Salad

Avocado and Lemon Salad

FRESH, SHARP LEMON JUICE GIVES THE PERFECT LIFT TO THIS ARRANGED GREEN SALAD. SERVE AS SOON AS POSSIBLE SO THAT THE COLOURS AND FLAVOURS ARE AT THEIR FRESHEST AND BEST

½ round lettuce, separated into leaves
about 75 g (3 oz) frisée or escarole, torn into pieces
¼ cucumber, cut into strips
125 g (4 oz) cooked green beans
1 bunch spring onions
2 ripe avocados
2 tablespoons lemon juice
1 lemon, sliced thinly
DRESSING:
3 tablespoons sunflower or walnut oil
1 tablespoon lemon juice
½ teaspoon grated lemon rind
1 teaspoon chopped mixed herbs (for example, parsley, chervil and thyme)
salt and pepper

Arrange the lettuce, frisée, cucumber, beans and spring onions attractively on a serving plate.

Peel, stone and slice the avocados and toss in the lemon juice to prevent them turning brown. Add to the serving plate and garnish with the lemon slices.

To make the dressing, beat the oil with the lemon juice, lemon rind, herbs and salt and pepper to taste until well blended. Spoon over the salad to coat. Serve at once.

SERVES 4-6

Nutritional content per serving: Carbohydrate: 6 g Fat: 37 g Fibre: 5 g Kilocalories: 380

Lamb's Lettuce with Spicy Dressing

LAMB'S LETTUCE IS A RATHER NEUTRAL-FLAVOURED YET TENDER SALAD LEAF THAT APPRECIATES THE FRUITY SPICINESS OF THIS DRESSING. SERVE AS A VERY SIMPLE APPETIZER SALAD OR WITH COLD BUFFET MEATS, FISH AND CHEESES AS A SIDE OR COMPLEMENTARY SALAD

500 g (1 lb) lamb's lettuce
4 tablespoons walnut or sunflower oil
2 tablespoons mango chutney
1 tablespoon lemon juice
1 tablespoon red wine vinegar
2 tablespoons chopped mixed herbs (for example, chives, lemon balm, mint and coriander)
salt and pepper
2 tablespoons pine kernels
mint leaves to garnish

Separate the lamb's lettuce into leaves, wash, dry, then place in a serving bowl.

To make the dressing, beat the oil with the mango chutney, lemon juice, vinegar, herbs and salt and pepper to taste until well blended. If the mixture seems a little too stiff then thin with a little more wine vinegar or lemon juice but take care not to make it too sharp.

Pour over the lamb's lettuce and toss gently to coat and mix. Sprinkle with the pine kernels, garnish with mint leaves and serve at once.

SERVES 4

Nutritional content per serving: Carbohydrate: 6 g Fat: 20 g Fibre: 4 g Kilocalories: 215

Lamb's Lettuce with Spicy Dressing; Avocado and Lemon Salad; Emerald Celeriac Salad

EMERALD CELERIAC SALAD

CELERIAC IS A MUCH UNDER-USED VEGETABLE, PERHAPS BECAUSE IT HAS SUCH AN UNATTRACTIVE APPEARANCE. ITS TASTE, HOWEVER, IS MOST DESIRABLE AND NOT UNLIKE CELERY. REMEMBER TO COOK IT WITH A LITTLE LEMON JUICE TO PREVENT IT TURNING BROWN. YOU CAN REPLACE THE SPINACH LEAVES WITH YOUNG SORREL WHEN AVAILABLE

1 large celeriac, peeled and diced
2 tablespoons lemon juice
about 175 g (6 oz) young spinach leaves
2 sticks celery, chopped
2 tablespoons chopped parsley
4 tablespoons Lemon Mayonnaise (see page 85)
2-3 tablespoons natural yogurt

Place the celeriac in a pan with a little salted water and the lemon juice. Bring to the boil and cook for 2 minutes. Drain thoroughly and allow to cool completely.

Transfer the celeriac to a serving bowl with the spinach, celery, and parsley. Toss gently to mix.

Mix the mayonniase with the yogurt to thin it a little then drizzle over the top of the salad. Serve as soon as possible.

SERVES 4

Nutritional content per serving: Carbohydrate: 4 g Fat: 12 g Fibre: 6 g Kilocalories: 136

Speckled Cucumber Salad; Tangy Grated Courgette Salad

TANGY GRATED COURGETTE SALAD

THIS IS A LAST-MINUTE SIDE SALAD TO MAKE JUST BEFORE SERVING. REPLACE THE TARRAGON WITH A LITTLE BASIL IF PREFERRED

5 medium young courgettes
1 tablespoon chopped tarragon
tarragon sprig to garnish
DRESSING:
3 tablespoons grapeseed or groundnut oil
grated rind of 1 lemon
4 tablespoons lemon juice
salt and pepper

Coarsely grate the courgettes into a sieve and drain thoroughly. Place in a bowl with the tarragon and toss to mix.

To make the dressing, beat the oil with the lemon rind, lemon juice and salt and pepper to taste until well blended. Pour over the courgette mixture and toss gently to coat and mix. Serve at once garnished with tarragon.

SERVES 4

Nutritional content per serving: Carbohydrate: 6 g Fat: 12 g Fibre: 0.5 g Kilocalories: 134

SPECKLED CUCUMBER SALAD

CHOOSE TARRAGON, DILL OR MINT TO COAT THE CUCUMBER IN THIS SALAD. IF USING TARRAGON THEN REPLACE 1 TEASPOON OF THE LEMON JUICE WITH TARRAGON VINEGAR

1 cucumber
small bunch of dill, tarragon or mint, chopped finely
4 tablespoons thick set natural yogurt
2 teaspoons lemon juice
2 shallots or small onions, chopped very finely
salt and pepper
sprigs of dill, tarragon or mint to garnish

Cut the cucumber into thin julienne strips and place in a bowl with the chosen chopped herbs.

Mix the yogurt with the lemon juice, shallots or onions and salt and pepper to taste. Stir into the cucumber mixture to coat and mix.

Serve the salad lightly chilled, garnished with sprigs of the chosen flavouring herb.

SERVES 4

Nutritional content per serving: Carbohydrate: 0.5 g Fat: 1 g Kilocalories: 27

MARINATED ASPARAGUS SALAD

NOTHING COULD BE NICER THAN SERVING FRESHLY COOKED, NEW-SEASON ASPARAGUS WITH A CREAMY MAYONNAISE SAUCE – BUT THIS MARINATED SALAD, WHICH CAN BE MADE WELL AHEAD FOR A SPECIAL-OCCASION STARTER, IS STIFF COMPETITION

about 750 g (1½ lb) asparagus spears
knob of butter
1 teaspoon tarragon vinegar
1 tablespoon orange juice
dash of vodka
salt and pepper
TO GARNISH:
chopped hard-boiled egg
parsley sprigs

Trim away any woody bases from the stems of the asparagus spears and peel if necessary. Place in a pan of boiling salted water with the butter, lower the heat and simmer until tender, about 20 minutes. Remove from the heat and leave to cool in the liquid.

Drain the asparagus, reserving 6 tablespoons of the cooking liquor. Mix the reserved liquor with the tarragon vinegar, orange juice, vodka and salt and pepper to taste. Pour over the asparagus and leave to marinate for at least 2 hours.

To serve, drain the asparagus from the marinade and place on a serving dish. Garnish with a little chopped hard-boiled egg and the parsley sprigs.

SERVES 4

Nutritional content per serving: Carbohydrate: 2 g Fat: 3 g Fibre: 2 g Kilocalories: 65

Marinated Asparagus Salad

WATERCRESS AND MUSHROOM SALAD

THIS SIMPLE MIXTURE IS A VERSATILE ANY-SEASON, ANY-OCCASION SALAD BUT IT IS ESPECIALLY GOOD WITH ROAST CHICKEN OR TURKEY, GAME BIRDS OR GRILLED WHOLE FISH LIKE SEA BASS

2 bunches watercress
175 g (6 oz) button mushrooms
2 spring onions, chopped, or 1 tablespoon snipped chives
DRESSING:
4 tablespoons soured cream
1 tablespoon Mayonnaise (see page 7)
1 teaspoon garlic purée
½ teaspoon celery seeds
salt and pepper

Place the watercress in a serving bowl. Add the mushrooms, left whole if small but sliced if larger, and spring onions or chives. Toss gently to mix.

To make the dressing, mix the soured cream with the mayonnaise, garlic purée, celery seeds and salt and pepper to taste. Drizzle over the salad to serve. Serve as soon as possible.

SERVES 4

Nutritional content per serving: Carbohydrate: 1 g Fat: 6 g Fibre: 3 g Kilocalories: 70

SUMMERHOUSE GREEN SALAD

MAKE THIS SALAD WITH THE VERY BEST OF THE SPRING AND SUMMER BOUNTY, CHOOSING THE FINEST YOUNG LEAFY GREEN VEGETABLES AND HERBS. ADD A HANDFUL OF GREEN BEANS, COOKED ASPARAGUS AND RADISH OR BEETROOT TOPS FOR VARIATION OR A FEW HERB FLOWERS TO INTRODUCE A DECORATIVE DASH OF COLOUR

½ head frisée or escarole, torn into pieces
about 50 g (2 oz) lamb's lettuce, separated into leaves
3 spring onions, chopped
1 bunch watercress or 1 punnet cress
about 50 g (2 oz) mangetout, blanched
1 medium courgette, cut into very thin slices or julienne strips
about a 5 cm (2 inch) piece of cucumber, sliced thinly
small handful of chopped mixed herbs, with their flowers if liked (for example, chives, rosemary, sage, borage, dill and fennel)
DRESSING:
3 tablespoons olive oil
1 tablespoon white wine vinegar
1 teaspoon flower-scented honey
¼ teaspoon Dijon mustard
salt and pepper

Place the frisée, lamb's lettuce, spring onions, watercress or cress, mangetout, courgette, cucumber and chopped mixed herbs in a large salad bowl.

To make the dressing, beat the oil with the vinegar, honey, mustard and salt and pepper to taste until well blended. Alternatively, place all the ingredients in a screw-top jar or bottle and shake vigorously to blend.

Pour over the salad just before serving and toss gently to coat and mix. Serve at once.

SERVES 4-6

Nutritional content per serving: Carbohydrate: 4 g Fat: 12 g Fibre: 3 g Kilocalories: 127

Summerhouse Green Salad; Watercress and Mushroom Salad; Pear Appetizer Salad

PEAR APPETIZER SALAD

THE PEARS AND AVOCADO FOR THIS SALAD SHOULD BE EQUALLY RIPE – THEY SHOULD GIVE JUST SLIGHTLY WHEN SQUEEZED. THE SOURED CREAM DRESSING CAN BE REPLACED WITH CHEESY LEMON DRESSING (SEE PAGE 94)

4 small ripe pears
1 ripe avocado
2 tablespoons lemon juice
½ punnet cress to garnish
DRESSING:
25 g (1 oz) curd cheese
5 tablespoons soured cream
2 spring onions, chopped finely
grated rind of ½ lemon
salt and pepper

Peel the pears if the skins are tough – if not, leave intact – then core and finely slice them. Peel, stone and slice the avocado. Toss the pear and avocado slices in the lemon juice to prevent them turning brown. Arrange on 4 small serving plates.

To make the dressing, beat the curd cheese with the soured cream, spring onions, lemon rind and salt and pepper to taste. Spoon a little on to each serving plate.

Garnish with a little cress and serve at once.

SERVES 4

Nutritional content per serving: Carbohydrate: 5 g Fat: 17 g Fibre: 2 g Kilocalories: 188

Greek Celery and Fennel Salad

Once made, this salad keeps well in the refrigerator for several days. Serve as part of a salad selection or with a variety of cold meats, salamis and paté

1 head celery, chopped into 5 cm (2 inch) pieces
2 heads fennel, cut into small wedge-shaped pieces
100 ml (3½ fl oz) water
100 ml (3½ fl oz) olive oil
4 tablespoons lemon juice
1 bay leaf
1 tablespoon chopped parsley
1 teaspoon chopped thyme
salt and pepper
TO GARNISH:
lemon slices, quartered
fennel fronds
bay leaf

Place the celery and fennel pieces in a large pan with the water, oil, lemon juice, bay leaf, parsley, thyme and salt and pepper to taste. Cover, bring to the boil, reduce the heat and simmer until tender, about 15 minutes, stirring occasionally. Remove from the heat and allow to cool.

Transfer to a serving dish, cover and leave to marinate for at least 4 hours. Drain away most of the marinade juices to serve.

Serve lightly chilled, garnished with lemon slices, fennel fronds and a bay leaf.

SERVES 4

Nutritional content per serving: Carbohydrate: 5 g Fat: 25 g Fibre: 6 g Kilocalories: 253

Chinese Leaf Salad

If you like a salad dressing with a bit of a kick, then add the finely chopped flesh of a small green chilli

1 small head Chinese leaves, cored and shredded finely
about 75 g (3 oz) fresh bean sprouts
6 canned water chestnuts, sliced finely
about 50 g (2 oz) canned bamboo shoots, sliced
2 tablespoons sesame seeds, toasted
DRESSING:
2 tablespoons sunflower oil
1 tablespoon sesame oil
1 tablespoon soy sauce
2 teaspoons lemon juice
1 teaspoon finely grated fresh root ginger
salt and pepper

Place the Chinese leaves, bean sprouts, water chestnuts, bamboo shoots and sesame seeds in a large serving bowl.

To make the dressing, beat the oils with the soy sauce, lemon juice, ginger and salt and pepper to taste until well blended. Alternatively, place all the ingredients in a screw-top jar and shake vigorously to blend.

Pour over the salad and toss gently to coat and mix. Serve as soon as possible.

SERVES 4

Nutritional content per serving: Carbohydrate: 9 g Fat: 15 g Fibre: 8 g Kilocalories: 206

Chinese Leaf Salad; Greek Celery and Fennel Salad; Frisée and Walnut Salad

FRISÉE AND WALNUT SALAD

WALNUT OIL IS THE IMPORTANT INGREDIENT IN THIS SALAD; NO OTHER OIL WILL GIVE QUITE THE SAME RESULT. THE MUSTARD CAN, HOWEVER, BE VARIED – EXPERIMENT WITH A VARIETY OF FLAVOURS; MUSTARD WITH GREEN PEPPERCORNS, GREEN HERB MUSTARD, FRENCH MUSTARD WITH TARRAGON OR COARSE GRAIN MUSTARD

2 heads frisée or escarole, torn into pieces
about 12 walnut halves
DRESSING:
3 tablespoons walnut oil
2 tablespoons sunflower or safflower oil
4 teaspoons red wine vinegar
1 teaspoon Dijon mustard
salt and pepper

Place the frisée in a large salad bowl. Crumble the walnut halves and add to the frisée.

To make the dressing, beat the oils with the vinegar, mustard and salt and pepper to taste until well blended. Alternatively, place all the ingredients in a screw-top jar or bottle and shake vigorously to blend.

Pour over the salad just before serving and toss gently to coat and mix. Serve at once.

SERVES 4-6

Nutritional content per serving: Carbohydrate: 3 g Fat: 29 g Fibre: 5 g Kilocalories: 290

Side salads

WHETHER YOU NEED A LIGHT SIDE SALAD DISH TO ACCOMPANY A SPICY CURRY, A BUBBLING PIZZA, A WARMING SOUP, A PLATTER OF COLD MEATS AND CHEESE OR A LUNCH BOX PASTRY OR PIE, THERE ARE MANY HERE TO FIT THE BILL. REMEMBER, TOO, THAT MANY OF THESE SALADS CAN BE SERVED AS A STARTER.

Apple, Avocado and Celery Pasta Salad

THIS FRESH, CRISP PASTA SALAD CAN BE MADE WITH ANY OF THE VARIOUS SMALL PASTA SHAPES – BOW-TIES, RINGS, WHEELS, SHELLS OR TWISTS. A GOOD SIDE SALAD TO SERVE WITH COLD ROAST MEAT OR POULTRY

250 g (8 oz) small pasta shapes
1 teaspoon vegetable oil
1 avocado
2 teaspoons lemon juice
3 sticks celery, chopped
1 red dessert apple, cored and sliced thinly
4 tablespoons French Dressing (see page 85)
2 tablespoons snipped chives

Cook the pasta shapes in boiling salted water with the oil, according to the packet instructions, until *al dente*. Drain and cool under cold water. Drain again thoroughly.

Peel and stone the avocado, then slice thinly or chop into cubes. Toss in the lemon juice to prevent it turning brown.

Mix the pasta with the avocado, celery and apple in a serving bowl. Add the dressing and chives and toss gently to coat and mix. Garnish with any extra chives.

SERVES 4-6

Nutritional content per serving: Carbohydrate: 54 g Fat: 26 g Fibre: 3 g Kilocalories: 480

Cauliflower, Bean and Rice Salad

THIS UNUSUAL SALAD MAKES A SPLENDID ADDITION TO ANY COLD TABLE SPREAD OR VEGETARIAN MEAL, AND IS PERFECT TO SERVE WITH SOUP AS A LIGHT BUT NUTRITIOUS LUNCH OR SUPPER MEAL

1 small cauliflower
125 g (4 oz) long-grain rice
125 g (4 oz) cooked red kidney beans
125 g (4 oz) cooked flageolet beans
1 tablespoon chopped mint
mint sprigs to garnish
DRESSING:
150 g (5.3 oz) carton natural yogurt
2 teaspoons natural bran
1 tablespoon lemon juice
1 small clove garlic, crushed
dash of Tabasco sauce
1 small onion, chopped finely
2 teaspoons chopped mint
salt and pepper

Trim the cauliflower into small florets. Cook in boiling salted water until just tender, about 6 minutes. Drain, refresh under cold running water, then drain again thoroughly.

Meanwhile, cook the rice in boiling salted water, according to the packet instructions, until tender. Drain thoroughly and allow to cool. Mix the cauliflower with the rice, beans and mint.

To make the dressing, mix the yogurt with the bran, lemon juice, garlic, Tabasco sauce, half the onion, half the mint and salt and pepper to taste. Fold into the cauliflower mixture. Spoon on to a serving dish and sprinkle with the remaining onion and mint. Garnish with the mint sprigs.

SERVES 4-6

Nutritional content per serving: Carbohydrate: 40 g Fat: 1 g Fibre: 8 g Kilocalories: 210

Apple, Avocado and Celery Pasta Salad; Cauliflower, Bean and Rice Salad

CALIFORNIAN POTATO SALAD

DON'T PEEL THE POTATOES FOR THIS SALAD; SIMPLY SCRUB THEM WELL BEFORE COOKING. SERVE THE SALAD EITHER WARM OR COLD

750 g (1½ lb) small new potatoes, scrubbed
125 g (4 oz) streaky bacon, derinded
125 g (4 oz) raisins
25 g (1 oz) cashew nuts
DRESSING:
4 tablespoons natural yogurt
50 g (2 oz) blue cheese, grated
1 teaspoon clear honey
salt and pepper

Boil or steam the potatoes in their skins, in or over boiling salted water until tender, about 15-20 minutes, depending upon size. Drain thoroughly and allow to cool if liked.

Grill the bacon until crisp, then crumble or chop coarsley. Mix the bacon with the potatoes and add the raisins.

To make the dressing, mix the yogurt with the cheese, honey and salt and pepper to taste. Add to the potato mixture and toss well to coat. Serve warm or cold, sprinkled with the cashew nuts.

Microwave: Place the potatoes in a bowl with 4 tablespoons cold water. Cover and microwave on Full Power for 8-10 minutes, until nearly tender. Leave to stand, covered, for 5 minutes, then drain thoroughly. Meanwhile, place the bacon on a plate or rack and cover with kitchen paper. Microwave on Full Power for 3½-4 minutes, then crumble or chop coarsely. Mix the potatoes with the bacon, raisins and dressing. Sprinkle with cashew nuts to serve.

SERVES 4-6

Nutritional content per serving: Carbohydrate: 59 g Fat: 18 g Fibre: 6 g Kilocalories: 432

SPICED COLESLAW

COLESLAW IS ANYTHING BUT ORDINARY WHEN MADE WITH THIS RICH, SPICY DRESSING. RING THE CHANGES OCCASIONALLY BY TOSSING THE RAW INGREDIENTS IN A BASIC MAYONNAISE (SEE PAGE 7) OR LEMON-FLAVOURED MAYONNAISE (SEE PAGE 85), THEN SPRINKLE WITH CARAWAY SEEDS INSTEAD OF CHOPPED PARSLEY

500 g (1 lb) white cabbage
1 onion, grated
2 carrots, grated
2 dessert apples, peeled, cored and grated
50 g (2 oz) walnut pieces
75 g (3 oz) mixed dried fruit (for example, apricots, dates, prunes and figs), chopped
4-5 tablespoons Curry Mayonnaise (see page 85)
1 tablespoon chopped parsley

Remove the tough outer leaves and core from the cabbage and shred finely into a large bowl. Add the onion, carrots, apples, walnuts and dried fruit.

Add the mayonnaise and toss gently to mix and coat. Spoon into a serving dish and sprinkle with the chopped parsley.

SERVES 6-8

Nutritional content per serving: Carbohydrate: 16 g Fat: 14 g Fibre: 6 g Kilocalories: 194

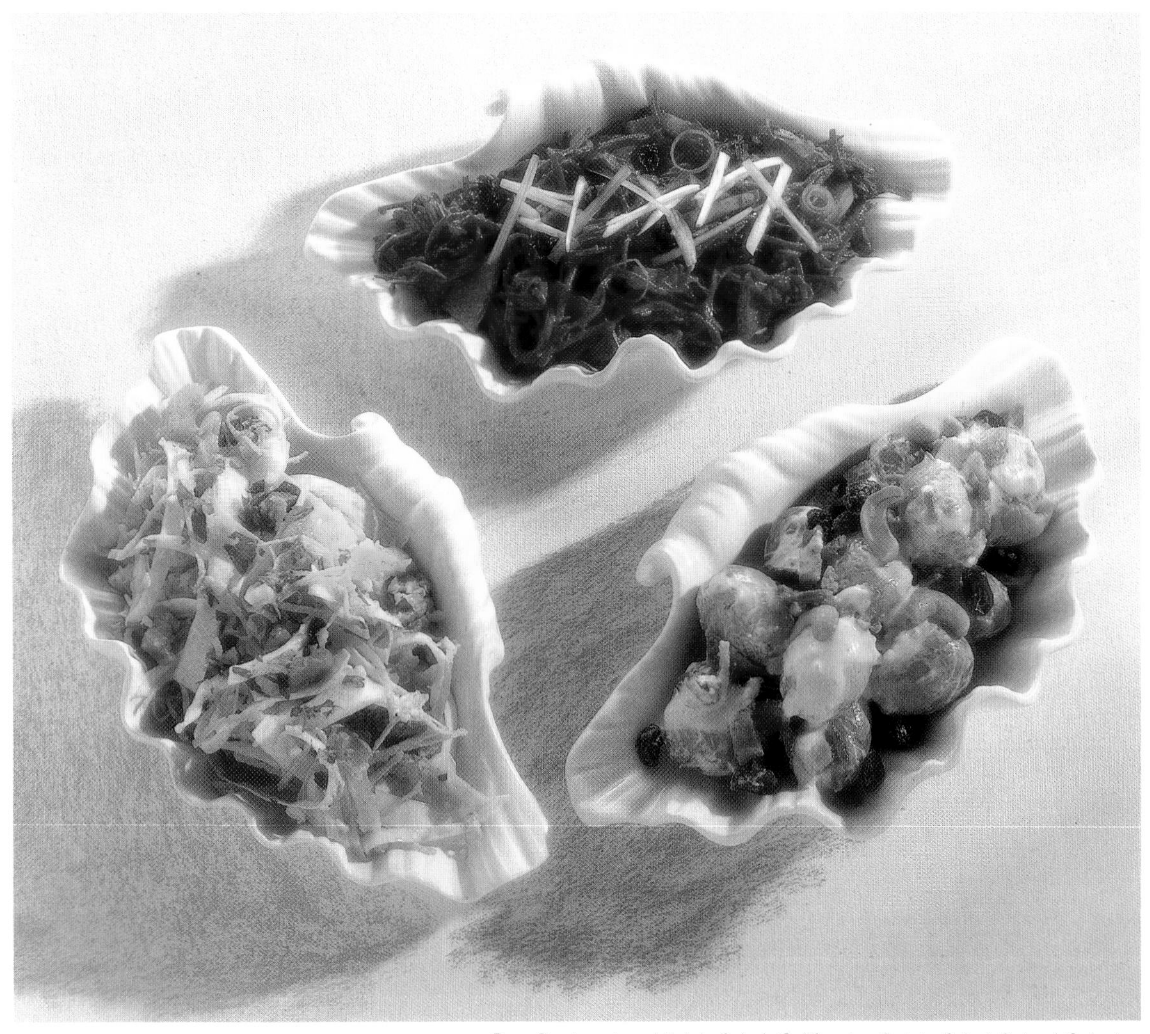

Raw Beetroot and Raisin Salad; Californian Potato Salad; Spiced Coleslaw

RAW BEETROOT AND RAISIN SALAD

THE RAW BEETROOT IN THIS SALAD PROVIDES A WONDERFUL CRISP TEXTURE AND A FLAVOUR THAT COMBINES WELL WITH APPLES, RAISINS AND SPRING ONIONS. IT IS WELL WORTH TRYING!

250 g (8 oz) raw young beetroot
3 spring onions, chopped
1 dessert apple, cored and chopped
125 g (4 oz) raisins
DRESSING:
150 g (5.3 oz) carton natural yogurt or soured cream
2 teaspoons creamed horseradish
salt and pepper

Peel the beetroot, then grate it coarsely into a bowl. Add half of the spring onions, the apple and raisins and mix well.

To make the dressing, mix the yogurt or soured cream with the horseradish and salt and pepper to taste. Fold into the beetroot mixture to blend and coat.

Serve lightly chilled, with the remaining chopped spring onions sprinkled on top.

SERVES 4-6

Nutritional content per serving: Carbohydrate: 30 g Fat: 1 g Fibre: 5 g Kilocalories: 136

Cheesy Fennel and Rice Salad; Marinated Mushroom and Orange Salad; Radish Sweet 'n' Sour

CHEESY FENNEL AND RICE SALAD

THIS IS A VERSATILE RICE AND VEGETABLE SALAD THAT CAN BE MADE USING A VARIETY OF CLEAR DRESSINGS – FRENCH (SEE PAGE 85), HONEY (SEE PAGE 86), RASPBERRY (SEE PAGE 89), OR MINT (SEE PAGE 87)

175 g (6 oz) long-grain rice
salt
4 tablespoons French Dressing (see page 85)
1 clove garlic, crushed
2 tablespoons chopped thyme
1 small head fennel, sliced thinly
1 red pepper, cored, deseeded and sliced
125 g (4 oz) button mushrooms, sliced
125 g (4 oz) Edam cheese, grated
fennel fronds to garnish

Cook the rice in boiling salted water, according to the packet instructions, until tender. Drain thoroughly and while still warm add the dressing, garlic and thyme. Mix well, cover and chill for 30 minutes.

Add the fennel, red pepper, mushrooms and cheese. Mix lightly to blend. Serve garnished with fennel fronds.

SERVES 4-6

Nutritional content per serving: Carbohydrate: 15 g Fat: 16 g Fibre: 2 g Kilocalories: 240

MARINATED MUSHROOM AND ORANGE SALAD

THIS TASTY SIDE SALAD WILL ALSO DOUBLE UP AS A LIGHT STARTER DISH FOR A SUBSTANTIAL MAIN MEAL, IN WHICH CASE IT SERVES 4. IT CAN BE MADE WELL IN ADVANCE AS IT WILL KEEP, REFRIGERATED IN AN AIRTIGHT CONTAINER, FOR UP TO 5 DAYS

2 tablespoons vegetable oil
150 ml (¼ pint) dry white wine
2 bay leaves
8 coriander seeds
1 large orange
750 g (1½ lb) button mushrooms
salt and pepper
TO GARNISH:
sprigs of dill
bay leaves

Place the oil, wine, bay leaves, coriander seeds and grated rind from the orange (reserving the flesh) in a large pan. Bring to the boil, add the mushrooms and cook gently until tender, about 5 minutes. Remove the mushrooms from their juices with a slotted spoon and place on individual plates.

Strain the cooking juices, season to taste and pour over the mushrooms. Remove the pith from the orange and cut the flesh into thin slices. Arrange on individual plates beside the mushrooms. Cover and cool, then chill for 6 hours or overnight.

Serve garnished with dill and bay leaves.

Microwave: Place the oil, wine, bay leaves, coriander seeds and grated rind from the orange (reserving the flesh) in a large bowl. Microwave on Full Power for 3 minutes. Add the mushrooms, cover and microwave on Medium – Full Power for 6 minutes, stirring once. Remove the mushrooms from their juices with a slotted spoon and place on individual plates. Strain the cooking juices, season to taste and pour over the mushrooms. Prepare and add the orange as above, cover, cool and chill before serving, garnished with dill and bay leaves.

SERVES 6

Nutritional content per serving: Carbohydrate: 2 g Fat: 6 g Fibre: 4 g Kilocalories: 71

RADISH SWEET 'N' SOUR

I OFTEN THROW A HANDFUL OF RADISHES INTO A MIXED SALAD FOR THEIR CRUNCHINESS, COLOURFUL APPEARANCE AND PEPPERY FLAVOUR, BUT THEY ALSO MAKE A SUPER SIDE SALAD DISH WHEN TOSSED IN A LITTLE SOY SAUCE-FLAVOURED DRESSING. IT IS IMPORTANT TO LET THE RADISHES MARINATE FOR A COUPLE OF HOURS. SERVINGS ARE SMALL AND ARE BEST PRESENTED AS PART OF A SELECTION OF SIDE SALADS WITH A COLD BUFFET-STYLE MEAL OR AT A BARBECUE

1 large bunch radishes
2 tablespoons sesame or sunflower oil
pinch of brown sugar
2 teaspoons soy sauce
1 tablespoon cider vinegar or lemon juice
1 teaspoon grated fresh root ginger
salt and pepper

Reserve a few radishes for garnishing. Slice the rest thinly and place in a bowl. Beat the oil with the sugar, soy sauce, vinegar or lemon juice, ginger and salt and pepper to taste. Pour over the radishes and toss gently to coat and mix. Cover the bowl and leave to marinate for at least 2 hours.

Stir again before serving, garnished with the reserved radishes.

SERVES 4

Nutritional content per serving: Carbohydrate: 2 g Fat: 8 g Fibre: 0.3 g Kilocalories: 79

SPEEDY BEANSLAW

THIS IS A QUICK AND EASY SIDE SALAD THAT IS POPULAR WITH CHILDREN. VARY THE INGREDIENTS FROM TIME TO TIME BY USING A CAN OF CURRIED BEANS INSTEAD OF THE FAVOURITE BEANS IN TOMATO SAUCE

250 g (8 oz) crisp white cabbage, shredded
447 g (15¾ oz) can beans in tomato sauce, drained of the sauce
3 carrots, grated
1 small onion, grated
2 sticks celery, chopped finely
50 g (2 oz) raisins
DRESSING:
5 tablespoons Mayonnaise (see page 7)
2 tablespoons sunflower oil
1 tablespoon white wine vinegar
salt and pepper

Mix the cabbage with the drained beans, carrots, onion, celery and raisins in a large bowl.

To make the dressing, mix the mayonnaise with the oil, vinegar and salt and pepper to taste. Fold into the salad mixture to coat and mix. Serve lightly chilled.

SERVES 6-8

Nutritional content per serving: Carbohydrate: 16 g Fat: 15 g Fibre: 8 g Kilocalories: 220

CHILLIED BEAN SPROUT SALAD

CHILLI LOVERS COULD INCREASE THE CHILLI POWDER IN THIS RECIPE TO 1 TEASPOON TO MAKE THE SALAD HOTTER AND MORE FIERY. SERVE WITH PLAIN COLD ROAST MEATS AND POULTRY AND, PERHAPS, A GREEN SALAD

250 g (8 oz) fresh bean sprouts
2 carrots, grated
50 g (2 oz) unsalted peanuts
1 bunch spring onions, chopped
125 g (4 oz) raisins
DRESSING:
6 tablespoons sunflower oil
½ teaspoon chilli powder
1 teaspoon soy sauce
1 teaspoon clear honey
2 tablespoons lemon juice
salt and pepper

Rinse the bean sprouts and drain thoroughly. Place in a bowl with the carrots, peanuts, spring onions and raisins.

To make the dressing, beat the oil with the chilli powder, soy sauce, honey, lemon juice and salt and pepper to taste until well blended. Alternatively, place all the ingredients in a screw-top jar and shake vigorously to blend.

Pour the dressing over the bean sprout mixture and toss gently to mix and coat.

SERVES 6

Nutritional content per serving: Carbohydrate: 19 g Fat: 19 g Fibre: 4 g Kilocalories: 260

Chillied Bean Sprout Salad; Alpine Salad; Speedy Beanslaw

ALPINE SALAD

THIS SIDE SALAD OF CRISP LETTUCE AND SWISS CHEESE WOULD ALSO MAKE A GOOD STARTER FOR A FORMAL MEAL OR LIGHT LUNCH DISH IF SERVED WITH CRUSTY FRENCH BREAD

- 175 g (6 oz) button mushrooms, sliced
- 6 tablespoons Chiffonade Dressing (see page 92) or French Dressing (see page 85)
- 175 g (6 oz) Swiss cheese (such as Gruyère or Emmenthal), diced
- 2 tablespoons snipped chives
- 4 large Cos lettuce leaves

Mix the mushrooms with the chosen dressing, cheese and chives. Cover and leave to stand for 10 minutes.

To serve, stir the cheese mixture to coat thoroughly in the dressing. Spoon equal amounts on to the lettuce leaves and place each leaf on a serving plate. Serve as soon as possible.

SERVES 4

Nutritional content per serving: Carbohydrate: 0.5 g Fat: 31 g Fibre: 2 g Kilocalories: 336

CRUNCHY PECAN AND ORANGE SPECIAL

WITH ITS SLICES OF FRESH, JUICY ORANGES, PECAN NUTS, FRISÉE AND CITRUS DRESSING, THIS SALAD MAKES AN IDEAL ACCOMPANIMENT TO A RICH DUCK OR GAME BIRD MAIN DISH

4 large oranges
about 125 g (4 oz) frisée or escarole, torn into pieces
about 50 g (2 oz) lamb's lettuce, separated into leaves
50 g (2 oz) pecan nuts
DRESSING:
4 tablespoons sunflower oil
3 tablespoons lemon juice
1 clove garlic, crushed
1 teaspoon finely grated orange rind
1 tablespoon chopped parsley
salt and pepper

Peel and remove the outer pith from the oranges. Using a sharp knife, carefully remove the orange segments. Remove any pips and place the orange segments in a serving dish. Add the frisée, lamb's lettuce and pecan nuts.

To make the dressing, beat the oil with the lemon juice, garlic, orange rind, parsley and salt and pepper to taste until well blended. Pour over the salad just before serving and toss gently to coat and mix.

SERVES 4

Nutritional content per serving: Carbohydrate: 11 g Fat: 21 g Fibre: 4 g Kilocalories: 245

Crunchy Pecan and Orange Special

Italian Pasta Salad

Italian Pasta Salad

Baby corn cobs make this pasta salad extra special, and the apple in the dressing gives it a tangy, piquant flavour

250 g (8 oz) small pasta shapes
1 teaspoon vegetable oil
175 g (6 oz) baby corn cobs
125 g (4 oz) raisins
1 red pepper, cored, deseeded and sliced
chives to garnish
DRESSING:
3 tablespoons Mayonnaise (see page 7)
3 tablespoons unsweetened apple purée
2 tablespoons snipped chives
salt and pepper

Cook the pasta shapes in boiling salted water with the oil, according to the packet instructions, until *al dente*. Drain and cool under cold water. Drain again thoroughly.

Meanwhile, cook the baby corn cobs in boiling salted water until just tender but still crisp, about 5 minutes. Drain thoroughly.

Mix the pasta with the baby corn cobs, raisins and red pepper in a serving bowl.

To make the dressing, mix the mayonnaise with the apple purée, chives and salt and pepper to taste. Fold into the pasta mixture to coat and mix. Garnish with chives.

SERVES 6

Nutritional content per serving: Carbohydrate: 48 g Fat: 8 g Fibre: 4 g Kilocalories: 278

HAWAIIAN RICE SALAD

THIS BRIGHT, VIBRANT, SUN-SOAKED FRUITY SALAD MAKES A WELCOME SIDE DISH TO A CURRY-FLAVOURED MAIN MEAL. IT IS ALSO DELICIOUS WITH PLAIN GRILLED FISH, WHEN THE ADDITION OF A LITTLE CHOPPED WATERCRESS GIVES IT A SUPERB PEPPERY FLAVOUR

175 g (6 oz) American long-grain rice
½ teaspoon ground turmeric
450 ml (¾ pint) vegetable stock
½ pineapple, peeled, cored and chopped
125 g (4 oz) sultanas
½ cucumber, cubed
1 small mango, peeled, stoned and sliced
DRESSING:
4 tablespoons lemon juice
2 tablespoons clear honey
2 tablespoons unsweetened pineapple juice
1 clove garlic, crushed
salt and pepper

Place the rice, turmeric, stock and salt to taste in a pan. Bring to the boil, reduce the heat, stir, then cover and simmer until tender, about 15 minutes. Drain thoroughly and allow to cool. Mix the rice with the pineapple, sultanas, cucumber and mango.

To make the dressing, beat the lemon juice with the honey, pineapple juice, garlic and salt and pepper to taste until well blended. Fold into the rice mixture.

SERVES 4-6

Nutritional content per serving: Carbohydrate: 78 g Fat: 1 g Fibre: 5 g Kilocalories: 317

TROPICAL SIDE SALAD

THIS IS A REFRESHING FRUITY SALAD COMBINATION TO SERVE WITH GRILLED FOOD, SLICED MEATS OR COLD PIES

1 small pineapple
1 red dessert apple, cored and chopped
3 sticks celery, chopped
75 g (3 oz) raisins
1 tablespoon pine kernels or sunflower seeds
25 g (1 oz) flaked coconut, toasted
DRESSING:
2 tablespoons Mayonnaise (see page 7)
2 tablespoons natural yogurt
salt and pepper

Peel and core the pineapple, then cut into bite-sized cubes. Place in a bowl with the apple, celery, raisins and pine kernels or sunflower seeds.

To make the dressing, mix the mayonnaise with the yogurt and salt and pepper to taste. Fold into the pineapple mixture to blend and coat. Serve lightly chilled, sprinkled with the toasted coconut.

SERVES 4

Nutritional content per serving: Carbohydrate: 31 g Fat: 10 g Fibre: 6 g Kilocalories: 219

Tropical Side Salad; Crunchy Date and Banana Salad; Hawaiian Rice Salad

CRUNCHY DATE AND BANANA SALAD

THIS SALAD COMBINATION IS JUST THE THING TO LIVEN UP JADED SUMMER APPETITES. IT IS ALSO AN UNUSUAL BUT GOOD SIDE SALAD TO ACCOMPANY A MILD CURRY DISH WITH ITS FRUITY FLAVOUR AND CRUNCHY TEXTURE

1 small or ½ medium cauliflower, broken into florets
50 g (2 oz) stoned dates, sliced thinly
2 bananas, sliced
2 tablespoons lemon juice
1 quantity Sherried Dressing (see page 90) or ½ quantity Soured Cream and Orange Dressing (see page 88)
salt and pepper
orange slices, halved, to garnish

Mix the cauliflower with the dates in a bowl. Toss the bananas in the lemon juice and add to the salad mixture.

Pour over the chosen dressing, add salt and pepper to taste and toss gently to coat and mix. Serve as soon as possible. Garnish with halved orange slices.

SERVES 4

Nutritional content per serving: Carbohydrate: 27 g Fat: 12 g Fibre: 5 g Kilocalories: 236

HERB CHEESE AND WALNUT SALAD

THE COMBINATION OF CRISP SALAD INGREDIENTS, FRUIT, NUTS AND CREAMY CHEESE IN THIS SALAD LIFTS A PLAIN MAIN MEAL DISH. YOU CAN DOUBLE THE CHEESE, FRUIT AND NUT QUANTITIES AND SERVE AS A LIGHT SALAD MEAL

1 small head frisée or escarole, chopped coarsely
1 head chicory, divided into spears
1 large orange, peeled, pith removed and chopped
125 g (4 oz) soft cheese with garlic and parsley
40 g (1½ oz) walnuts, chopped finely
DRESSING:
4 tablespoons grapeseed oil
2 tablespoons red wine vinegar
½ teaspoon Dijon mustard
salt and pepper

Place the frisée and the chicory spears on individual dishes. Scatter the orange pieces over them.

Cream the cheese to soften, then divide and shape into small balls and roll in the walnuts to coat evenly. Pile on top of the orange and frisée mixture.

To make the dressing, beat the oil with the vinegar, mustard and salt and pepper to taste until well blended. Spoon over the salads just before serving.

SERVES 4

Nutritional content per serving: Carbohydrate: 5 g Fat: 35 g Fibre: 3 g Kilocalories: 349

FRESNO BEAN SALAD

CANNED TOMATOES MAY BE USED TO MAKE THE DRESSING FOR THIS COLOURFUL BEAN SALAD WHEN PLUMP, RIPE SUMMER TOMATOES ARE NOT AVAILABLE. IT IS A PERFECT COOK-AHEAD SALAD SINCE IT WILL KEEP IN THE REFRIGERATOR FOR UP TO 5 DAYS

400 g (14 oz) can red kidney beans, drained
400 g (14 oz) can chick-peas, drained
125 g (4 oz) raisins
125 g (4 oz) button mushrooms, sliced
1 green pepper, cored, deseeded and chopped
1 small onion, chopped finely
2 sticks celery, chopped
2 tablespoons chopped parsley
DRESSING:
250 g (8 oz) ripe tomatoes
2 tablespoons olive oil
1 clove garlic, crushed
1 teaspoon paprika
salt and pepper

Rinse the beans and chick-peas in cold water and drain thoroughly. Place in a large salad bowl with the raisins, mushrooms, green pepper, onion, celery and parsley.

To make the dressing, place the tomatoes in a bowl and cover with boiling water. Leave to stand for 1 minute, then drain and remove the skins. Halve and deseed the tomatoes, then finely chop the flesh. Place in a bowl with the oil, garlic, paprika and salt and pepper to taste, mixing well.

Stir the dressing into the bean mixture and toss gently to mix and coat. Cover and chill until ready to serve. Stir well before serving.

SERVES 6-8

Nutritional content per serving: Carbohydrate: 35 g Fat: 7 g Fibre: 11 g Kilocalories: 232

Fresno Bean Salad; Herb Cheese and Walnut Salad; Tomato and Basil Salad

TOMATO AND BASIL SALAD

FOR AUTHENTICITY MAKE THIS SIDE SALAD ONLY WITH RIPE, PLUMP EXTRA LARGE TOMATOES, BASIL AND THE VERY BEST ITALIAN VIRGIN OLIVE OIL – ANYTHING LESS REALLY DOESN'T PRODUCE THE SAME RESULTS. ITALIAN BALSAMIC VINEGAR CAN BE USED INSTEAD OF RED WINE VINEGAR – ITS DEEP, RICH AND LONG-MATURED FLAVOUR IS WONDERFUL WITH TOMATOES

4 extra large ripe tomatoes
¼ small onion, grated
about 4 sprigs basil, finely chopped
4 tablespoons virgin olive oil
1 tablespoon red wine vinegar
salt and pepper
basil sprigs to garnish

Thinly slice the tomatoes on to a large serving plate. Scatter over the onion and chopped basil.

Just before serving, add the oil, vinegar and salt and pepper to taste, and toss gently to coat and mix. Serve at once, garnished with basil sprigs.

SERVES 4

Nutritional content per serving: Carbohydrate: 7 g Fat: 15 g Fibre: 3 g Kilocalories: 168

Stuffed Nasturtium Flower Salad

NASTURTIUM FLOWERS FROM THE GARDEN ARE OFTEN USED AS JUST A GARNISH OR DECORATION FOR SUMMER SALADS AND DESSERTS. THIS IS ONE OF THE MORE INTERESTING WAYS I HAVE FOUND OF SERVING THEM, WHERE THEIR USE IS MORE FUNDAMENTAL THAN DECORATIVE. IT MAKES AN INTRIGUING STARTER TO A HEARTY MAIN MEAL OR CAN BE TREATED AS PART OF A SIDE SALAD SELECTION

16 nasturtium flowers and their leaves
3 tablespoons Raspberry Dressing (see page 89)
4 hard-boiled eggs
2 tablespoons Lemon Mayonnaise (see page 85)
1 tablespoon chopped parsley
1 tablespoon snipped chives
salt and pepper

Carefully remove the flowers and strip the leaves from the stems of the nasturtiums, and rinse. Arrange the leaves on 4 shallow plates and drizzle over the raspberry dressing.

Shell and mash the eggs with a fork. Add the mayonnaise, parsley, chives and salt and pepper to taste, mixing well. Fill the nasturtium flowers with this mixture and arrange decoratively on top of the dressed leaves. Serve as soon as possible.

SERVES 4

Nutritional content per serving: Carbohydrate: 0.5 g Fat: 20 g Fibre: 0.5 g Kilocalories: 213

Continental Side Salad

THIS STYLISH SIDE SALAD DOES NOT HAVE ANY FIXED INGREDIENTS – INCLUDE THE VERY BEST OF UNUSUAL SEASONAL SALAD PRODUCE, EXOTIC FRESH FRUITS AND NUTS AS SURPRISE ADDITIONS WHEN AVAILABLE IN THE SHOPS

50 g (2 oz) frisée or escarole, torn into pieces
25 g (1 oz) feuille de chêne or quattro stagione, torn into pieces
25 g (1 oz) radicchio, torn into pieces
25 g (1 oz) lamb's lettuce, separated into leaves
1 ripe avocado or pear
2 teaspoons lemon juice
1 large fresh peach or nectarine
25 g (1 oz) almonds or pine kernels, toasted
5 tablespoons French Dressing (see page 85) or Raspberry Dressing (see page 89)
1 tablespoon chopped mixed herbs (for example, chives, parsley, sage and tarragon)

Place the frisée, feuille de chêne, radicchio and lamb's lettuce in a serving bowl and toss lightly to mix.

Peel, stone and thinly slice the avocado, then toss in the lemon juice to prevent it turning brown, or slice the pear. Stone and slice the peach. Add the avocado or pear and peach to the salad mixture with the nuts.

Pour the dressing over the salad and scatter over the herbs. Toss gently to mix and coat before serving.

SERVES 4

Nutritional content per serving: Carbohydrate: 4 g Fat: 28 g Fibre: 3 g Kilocalories: 286

Leek and Pepper Vinaigrette; Stuffed Nasturtium Flower Salad; Continental Side Salad

LEEK AND PEPPER VINAIGRETTE

WHEN SALAD LEAVES ARE EXPENSIVE DURING THE WINTER MONTHS, LEEKS COME AS A WELCOME ADDITION TO THE SALAD BOWL. COMBINED WITH PEPPERS, ALMONDS AND A CLEAR DRESSING THEY MAKE A GOOD ACCOMPANIMENT FOR ALMOST ANY MAIN MEAL DISH

3 medium leeks
½ red pepper, cored, deseeded and sliced
1 teaspoon finely grated lemon rind
5 tablespoons Citrus Vinaigrette (see Classic Vinaigrette, page 85)
2 tablespoons flaked almonds

Very finely shred the leeks and blanch them in boiling water for 2 minutes. Drain and refresh under cold running water, then drain again thoroughly.

Mix the leeks with the red pepper, lemon rind and dressing, tossing well to coat and mix. Spoon into a serving bowl and scatter with the almonds to serve.

SERVES 4

Nutritional content per serving: Carbohydrate: 10 g Fat: 15 g Fibre: 6 g Kilocalories: 190

Carrot and couscous salad

This side salad can be made with bulgar wheat instead of couscous. It is a good dish to make ahead of time and will keep in the refrigerator for 3-4 days. Serve as part of a salad selection

250 g (8 oz) couscous
2 large carrots, grated
½ red onion, chopped finely
½ quantity Basic Mayonnaise (see page 7) or Herb Mayonnaise (see page 85)
salt and pepper
red onion rings to garnish

Place the couscous in a dish and moisten with warm water. Stand for 10 minutes. Place in a strainer or metal sieve and steam over boiling water for 15 minutes or until soft. Allow to cool. Place the cooked couscous, carrots and onion in a bowl and stir to mix. Add the chosen mayonnaise with salt and pepper to taste. Toss gently to coat and mix. Cover and chill until required. Stir again to mix before serving. Garnish with red onion rings.

SERVES 4-6

Nutritional content per serving: Carbohydrate: 34 g Fat: 44 g Fibre: 1 g Kilocalories: 547

Alfalfa salad

Sprouted alfalfa mixed with cress and a creamy dressing makes a more unusual summer side salad than traditional coleslaw. Add a few poppy seeds, sunflower seeds or a dusting of spices for variety

about 250 g (8 oz) sprouted alfalfa
1 punnet cress
1 carrot, grated coarsely
6 tablespoons Normandy Dressing (see page 91) or Yogurt Dressing (see page 93)
pinch of chilli powder
pinch of paprika

Mix the alfalfa with the trimmed cress and the carrot in a large bowl. Add the chosen dressing and toss to coat and mix.

Spoon into a serving bowl and dust with the chilli powder and paprika to serve.

SERVES 4

Nutritional content per serving: Carbohydrate: 5g Fat: 9 g Fibre: 1 g Kilocalories: 107

Winter mooli salad

Mooli is a winter radish, usually white in colour (but sometimes brown, purple or even black) and much larger than the traditional red summer radish. It does, however, have the same mild peppery flavour and taste

1 large mooli, peeled
125 ml (4 fl oz) soured cream
2 tablespoons unsweetened apple purée
salt
2 teaspoons snipped chives

Coarsely grate the mooli, place in a sieve and sprinkle with salt. Leave to stand for 15 minutes, then rinse and dry thoroughly.

Mix with the soured cream and apple purée, blending well. Spoon into a serving dish and sprinkle with the chives. Serve as soon as possible.

SERVES 4

Nutritional content per serving: Carbohydrate: 6 g Fat: 6 g Fibre: 1 g Kilocalories: 83

Alfalfa Salad; Carrot and Couscous Salad; Winter Mooli Salad

Hot and Warm Salads

Nothing is more beguiling than a hot or warm salad, whether you choose a simple green salad topped with a creamy warm dressing; a hastily but delicately tossed salad of warm bacon or chicken livers with leaves; or a steamy offering of scrubbed new potatoes in a sharp dressing.

FRUITY RICE SALAD

ALTHOUGH THIS FRUIT-LADEN RICE SALAD IS DELICIOUS SERVED WARM, IT IS EQUALLY GOOD COLD. PRESENT IT AS PART OF A VEGETARIAN-STYLE MEAL OR COLD, AS HEARTY PICNIC FARE ON SUMMER DAYS

250 g (8 oz) long-grain brown rice
450 ml (¾ pint) unsweetened apple juice
450 ml (¾ pint) cold water
1 red pepper, cored, deseeded and chopped
1 orange, peeled, pith removed and chopped
25 g (1 oz) dried apricots, chopped
4 spring onions, chopped
2 tablespoons chopped parsley
3 tablespoons French Dressing (see page 85)
parsley sprigs to garnish

Rinse the rice several times in cold water. Place in a pan with the apple juice and water. Bring to the boil, reduce the heat, partially cover and simmer until tender and all the liquid has been absorbed, about 30-40 minutes.

Add the red pepper, orange, apricots, spring onions, parsley and French dressing. Toss gently to mix and coat. Serve at once while still warm garnished with parsley sprigs.

Microwave: Place the rice in a bowl with 300 ml (½ pint) unsweetened apple juice and 300 ml (½ pint) boiling water. Cover and microwave on Full Power for 3 minutes. Reduce the power setting to Medium and microwave for a further 25 minutes, stirring twice. Add the red pepper, orange, apricots, spring onions, parsley and French dressing. Toss gently to mix and coat. Serve at once while still warm.

SERVES 4-6

Nutritional content per serving: Carbohydrate: 74 g Fat: 10 g Fibre: 5 g Kilocalories: 400

BLUTO'S REVENGE

POPEYE NEVER TASTED SPINACH SO GOOD! THIS SALAD IS PERFECT FOR A LIGHT LUNCH OR IT MAKES A STARTER DISH

about 375 g (12 oz) young spinach leaves
2 hard-boiled eggs
small handful of garlic croûtons (see page 95)
125 g (4 oz) smoked bacon, derinded and chopped
2 tablespoons olive oil
2 tablespoons lemon juice
½ teaspoon Dijon mustard
salt and pepper

Make sure the spinach leaves are thoroughly rinsed and dry, then tear and place in a serving bowl. Shell and coarsely chop the eggs and add to the spinach with the garlic croûtons.

Fry the bacon in a frying pan without any additional fat until crisp, brown and all the bacon fat has been released. Remove with a slotted spoon, drain on kitchen paper, then add to the salad mixture.

Add the oil, lemon juice, mustard and salt and pepper to the bacon fat and stir well to blend. Quickly pour over the salad and toss gently to coat and mix. Serve at once while the bacon is still warm.

SERVES 4

Nutritional content per serving: Carbohydrate: 6 g Fat: 24 g Fibre: 1 g Kilocalories: 283

Fruity Rice Salad; Bluto's Revenge

Hot Kiwi, Pasta and Bacon Salad; Warm Minted Potato and Cucumber Salad

WARM MINTED POTATO AND CUCUMBER SALAD

THIS VERSATILE WARM SALAD IS AN ANY-SEASON DISH. SERVE AS PART OF A COLD BUFFET SPREAD, BARBECUE MEAL OR WITH COLD MEAT

500 g (1 lb) new potatoes
¼ cucumber, sliced thinly
4 tablespoons Mint Dressing (see page 87)
salt
mint sprigs to garnish

Scrape the potatoes or scrub well. Boil or steam them, in or over boiling salted water until tender, about 15-20 minutes, depending upon size. Drain thoroughly.

While still warm, mix with the cucumber and dressing, and toss well to coat. Serve at once, garnished with mint sprigs.

SERVES 4

Nutritional content per serving: Carbohydrate: 24 g Fat: 11 g Fibre: 3 g Kilocalories: 203

HOT KIWI, PASTA AND BACON SALAD

THIS HOT SALAD DISH NEEDS LITTLE LAST MINUTE ATTENTION. SERVE, IF LIKED, WITH A VERY SIMPLE GREEN SALAD

250 g (8 oz) tagliatelle
1 teaspoon vegetable oil
4 kiwi fruit, peeled and sliced thickly
8 rashers back bacon, derinded and chopped
2 tablespoons white wine vinegar
pepper
chopped parsley to garnish

Cook the tagliatelle in boiling salted water with the oil, according to the packet instructions, until *al dente*. Drain thoroughly and place in a serving dish with the kiwi fruit. Keep warm.

Meanwhile, fry the bacon in a frying pan without any additional fat until crisp and golden. Add the vinegar to the pan, bring to the boil, then pour over the pasta. Season with pepper and toss gently to coat and mix.

Garnish with parsley and serve at once while the bacon mixture is still hot.

SERVES 4

Nutritional content per serving: Carbohydrate: 56 g Fat: 24 g Fibre: 5 g Kilocalories: 470

WARM CHICKEN LIVER AND GRAPE SALAD

TENDER CHICKEN LIVERS MAKE A WONDERFUL WARM SALAD INGREDIENT WHEN TOSSED WITH GRAPES IN A MUSTARDY DRESSING

50 g (2 oz) butter
1 tablespoon safflower oil
500 g (1 lb) chicken livers, halved
1 teaspoon wholegrain mustard (Moutarde de Meaux)
2 tablespoons Marsala wine or medium dry sherry
2 teaspoons white wine vinegar
250 g (8 oz) seedless white grapes
1 small feuille de chêne or quattro stagione
salt and pepper
2 tablespoons chopped parsley

Heat the butter and oil in a frying pan. Add the chicken livers and fry gently until cooked but still pink, about 3 minutes.

Add the mustard, wine and vinegar, blending well. Stir in the grapes with salt and pepper to taste and toss gently until hot.

Meanwhile, line a serving plate with the feuille de chêne leaves. Spoon the chicken liver and grape mixture on top. Sprinkle with parsley and serve at once while still warm, with toast triangles.

SERVES 4

Nutritional content per serving: Carbohydrate: 12 g Fat: 22 g Fibre: 2 g Kilocalories: 352

Warm Chicken Liver and Grape Salad

WARM MELON AND PRAWN SCOOPS

THIS SPECIAL STARTER IS BEST MADE WITH SMALL CANTALOUPE MELONS THAT HAVE FRAGRANT, SWEET ORANGE FLESH. THE DISH IS ESPECIALLY EASY TO PREPARE IF YOU HAVE A MICROWAVE OVEN

2 small cantaloupe melons
125 g (4 oz) peeled prawns
3 tablespoons Raspberry Dressing (see page 89)
1 teaspoon Crème de Cassis liqueur
¼ teaspoon wholegrain mustard (Moutarde de Meaux)
TO GARNISH:
1 tablespoon chopped coriander or parsley
prawns in shells (optional)

Halve each melon, then remove and discard the seeds. Using a melon baller or teaspoon, scoop out the flesh in small balls. Return them to the shells and wrap tightly in foil. Cook in a preheated oven, 180°C, 350°F, Gas Mark 4, for 5-10 minutes until warm.

Meanwhile, mix the prawns with the dressing, Crème de Cassis and mustard.

Remove the melons from the oven, unwrap and place each in a serving dish. Alternatively, turn out the melon balls into individual serving dishes.

Spoon over an equal quantity of the prawn and dressing mixture and stir gently into the melon balls to coat. Garnish with chopped coriander or parsley and prawns, if using, and serve at once while the melon is still warm.

Microwave: Prepare the melon halves as above but do not wrap in foil. Place in small serving dishes in the oven and microwave, uncovered, on Full Power for 2 minutes until hot. Add the prawn mixture, toss and serve as above.

SERVES 4

Nutritional content per serving: Carbohydrate: 12 g Fat: 8 g Fibre: 2 g Kilocalories: 158

GREEK POMEGRANATE SALAD

POMEGRANATES ARE GOOD LUCK SYMBOLS IN GREECE. THIS SALAD USES THEM MOST EFFECTIVELY, COMBINING THEM WITH CHINESE LEAVES, THOUGH FOR A SHARPER FLAVOUR YOU CAN USE WHITE CABBAGE INSTEAD. SERVE WITH GREEK FETA CHEESE

500 g (1 lb) Chinese leaves, shredded finely
4 tablespoons Honey Dressing (see page 86)
1 large ripe pomegranate
salt and pepper

Place the Chinese leaves in a large serving bowl. Place the dressing in a small saucepan with juice from half of the pomegranate. Heat gently until warm but do not allow to evaporate.

Remove the seeds from the remaining half of the pomegranate and scatter over the cabbage. Pour over the warm dressing with salt and pepper to taste and toss gently to coat and mix.

Serve at once.

SERVES 4

Nutritional content per serving: Carbohydrate: 14 g Fat: 5 g Fibre: 3 g Kilocalories: 110

Exotic Tropics Salad; Warm Melon and Prawn Scoops; Greek Pomegranate Salad

EXOTIC TROPICS SALAD

SPEED AND DEFTNESS OF HAND ARE THE SECRET TO PRODUCING THIS SALAD SUCCESSFULLY. THE WARM CURRY DRESSING ADDS BRILLIANT COLOUR AS WELL AS FLAVOUR. SERVE WITH CRISP SPICED PUPPADUMS

2 ripe mangoes, peeled
2 ripe peaches, peeled
2 tablespoons grapeseed oil
1 teaspoon grated fresh root ginger
5 tablespoons Raspberry Dressing (see page 89)
1 teaspoon garam masala or mild curry powder
coriander or parsley sprigs to garnish

Slice the mango flesh from the stones and cut into thin slices. Halve the peaches and remove the stones; slice the peaches thinly.

Heat the oil in a large non-stick pan until hot. Add the mango and peach slices and cook gently until hot but not fallen, about 1-2 minutes. Remove carefully with a slotted spoon and arrange on 4 individual serving dishes.

Quickly stir the ginger, dressing and garam masala into the pan juices and stir until hot and blended. Drizzle over the salad and serve at once while still warm. Garnish with coriander or parsley sprigs.

SERVES 4

Nutritional content per serving: Carbohydrate: 15 g Fat: 20 g Fibre: 2 g Kilocalories: 239

HOT POTATO SALAD

THIS IS JUST THE WARMING ACCOMPANIMENT TO SERVE AT A BARBECUE WHEN THE WEATHER DOESN'T LIVE UP TO EXPECTATIONS AND GREEN SALAD FINERY SEEMS A CHILLY PROSPECT!

750 g (1½ lb) small waxy potatoes, scrubbed
2 large dill pickles, sliced finely
3 hard-boiled eggs, chopped
1 red pepper, cored, deseeded and sliced
2 tablespoons French Dressing (see page 85)
4 tablespoons Mayonnaise (see page 7) or Roquefort and Chive Dressing (see page 95)
2 tablespoons snipped chives
salt and pepper
chives to garnish

Boil or steam the potatoes in their skins, in or over boiling salted water until tender, about 15-20 minutes, depending upon size. Drain thoroughly, cut into bite-sized pieces and keep warm.

Add the dill pickles, eggs and red pepper to the warm potatoes. Mix the French dressing with the mayonnaise or roquefort and chive dressing, chives and salt and pepper to taste. Pour over the salad and toss gently to coat and mix.

Serve the salad while still warm garnished with chives.

SERVES 4-6

Nutritional content per serving: Carbohydrate: 37 g Fat: 23 g Fibre: 5 g Kilocalories: 398

PROVENÇAL BAKED TOMATO AND PEPPER SALAD

THIS CRUSTY BAKED TOMATO AND PEPPER SALAD IS EQUALLY DELICIOUS SERVED WARM OR COLD. USE A GOOD SELECTION OF FRESH HERBS OR A FRAGRANT MIXTURE OF DRIED *HERBES DE PROVENCE* (PARSLEY, SAGE, THYME, ROSEMARY AND BAY LEAVES MIXED). IF SERVING CHILLED YOU CAN TOP THE SALAD WITH A LATTICE OF ANCHOVY FILLETS.

4 extra large tomatoes, sliced
2 red peppers, cored, deseeded and cut into thin strips
4 tablespoons olive oil
½ clove garlic, crushed
2 tablespoons chopped mixed herbs (for example, basil, thyme, rosemary and parsley) or 2 teaspoons dried herbes de Provence
2 tablespoons fresh white breadcrumbs
salt and pepper

Layer the tomatoes and peppers in a small ovenproof dish, seasoning between each layer with olive oil, garlic, herbs and salt and pepper to taste, finishing with a layer of tomatoes.

Sprinkle with the breadcrumbs and bake in a preheated oven, 220°C, 425°F, Gas Mark 7, for about 20-25 minutes, until the top is browned and crisp.

Serve warm, or allow to cool then cover and chill.

SERVES 4-6

Nutritional content per serving: Carbohydrate: 15 g Fat: 16 g Fibre: 4 g Kilocalories: 243

Hot Potato Salad; Goat's Cheese Salad; Provençal Baked Tomato and Pepper Salad

Goat's cheese salad

The perfect alfresco dish, this bread and goat's cheese salad needs to be eaten as soon as it's made

1 small iceberg lettuce, torn into pieces
a few leaves of radicchio, torn into pieces
6 slices French bread
125 g (4 oz) goat's cheese
DRESSING:
4 tablespoons grapeseed oil
1 tablespoon white wine vinegar
½ teaspoon celery seeds
salt and pepper

Place the lettuce and radicchio in a large salad bowl. Toast one side of each French bread slice until golden. Slice the cheese into rounds and place a slice on top of each untoasted side of the bread. Place under a preheated hot grill and toast until the cheese is just melting.

Meanwhile, to make the dressing, beat the oil with the vinegar, celery seeds and salt and pepper to taste until well blended. Pour over the lettuce mixture and toss to mix and coat.

Cut each slice of cheesy bread in half and add to the salad. Toss gently to mix. Serve at once while still warm.

SERVES 4

Nutritional content per serving: Carbohydrate: 23 g Fat: 22 g Fibre: 3 g Kilocalories: 327

DEEP SOUTH PRAWN AND FISH SALAD

MAKE THIS WARM FISH SALAD WITH HUSS WHEN AVAILABLE. IT HAS FIRM PINK FLESH AND A DELICIOUS, IF MILD, FLAVOUR. WHEN YOU CAN'T FIND IT, USE MONKFISH, HALIBUT OR ANY OTHER WHITE FISH WITH A FIRM, COMPACT FLESH

375 g (12 oz) monkfish, halibut or huss fillet, skinned, boned and cubed
1 tablespoon lemon juice
about 150 ml (¼ pint) water
1 bay leaf
500 g (1 lb) tiny new potatoes, scrubbed
¼ cucumber, sliced thinly
175 g (6 oz) peeled prawns
2 tablespoons salted peanuts, chopped
DRESSING:
2 tablespoons crunchy peanut butter
¼ teaspoon wholegrain mustard (Moutarde de Meaux)
3 tablespoons boiling water
salt and pepper

Poach the fish in the lemon juice and water with the bay leaf until just tender, about 5 minutes. Drain thoroughly.

Meanwhile, boil or steam the potatoes in their skins, in or over boiling salted water until tender, about 15-20 minutes, depending upon size. Drain thoroughly.

Mix the potatoes with the fish, cucumber, prawns and peanuts and place in a warmed serving bowl.

To make the dressing, mix the peanut butter with the mustard, water and salt and pepper to taste. Spoon over the warm salad and serve at once.

Microwave: Place the fish, lemon juice, water and bay leaf in a bowl, cover and microwave on Full Power for 3-4 minutes, stirring once, until just cooked. Leave to stand while cooking the potatoes. Place the potatoes in a bowl with 4 tablespoons cold water. Cover and microwave on Full Power for 6-8 minutes, until nearly tender. Leave to stand, covered, for 5 minutes, then drain thoroughly. To serve, drain the fish and potatoes and mix with the cucumber, prawns and peanuts. Prepare the dressing as above and spoon over the salad.

SERVES 4

Nutritional content per serving: Carbohydrate: 25 g Fat: 13 g Fibre: 4 g Kilocalories: 359

JAPANESE TOFU SALAD

TOFU (BEAN CURD) IS ONE OF THOSE HIGHLY NUTRITIOUS FOODS THAT DESERVE MUCH MORE ATTENTION. FRIED HERE IN SESAME OIL AND MIXED WITH TOMATOES AND CUCUMBER, IT SHOULD WHET YOUR APPETITE FOR FURTHER EXPERIMENTS

1 extra large tomato, chopped
½ cucumber, cut into julienne strips
3 tablespoons sesame oil
250 g (8 oz) firm tofu (bean curd), cubed
1 shallot, small onion or spring onion, chopped finely
1 teaspoon sesame seeds, toasted
2 teaspoons white wine vinegar
salt and pepper

Mix the tomato with the cucumber and place on a large shallow serving plate.

Heat the oil in a frying pan, add the tofu cubes and fry until browned on all sides, about 2-3 minutes. Remove with a slotted spoon and keep warm.

Stir the shallot or onion and sesame seeds into the pan juices and cook for 1 minute. Add the vinegar with salt and pepper to taste and warm gently.

To serve, scatter the fried tofu over the tomato and cucumber mixture and drizzle over the hot dressing. Serve at once while the tofu is still warm.

SERVES 4

Nutritional content per serving: Carbohydrate: 3 g Fat: 14 g Fibre: 1 g Kilocalories: 163

Deep South Prawn and Fish Salad; Fried Bean and Nut Salad; Japanese Tofu Salad

FRIED BEAN AND NUT SALAD

YOU COULD, OF COURSE, USE ANY MIXTURE OF COOKED BEANS FOR THIS SALAD – BLACK, BORLOTTI OR FLAGEOLET BEANS ARE GOOD ALTERNATIVES TO THOSE CHOSEN HERE

75 g (3 oz) aduki beans, soaked overnight
75 g (3 oz) black-eye beans, soaked overnight
4 tablespoons safflower oil
1 clove garlic, crushed
about 75 g (3 oz) red or white cabbage, cored and shredded
2 tablespoons salted cashew nuts
1 tablespoon red wine vinegar
2 tablespoons chopped parsley
salt and pepper
parsley sprigs to garnish

Drain the beans, place in a pan and cover with cold water. Bring to a rapid boil, reduce the heat, cover and simmer until tender, about 45 minutes, adding a little salt towards the end of the cooking time. Drain thoroughly.

Heat the oil in a large, deep frying pan and fry the garlic for 1 minute but do not allow to brown. Add the beans and fry lightly for 2-3 minutes.

Add the cabbage and nuts, blending well, and stir-fry for 2 minutes. Stir in the vinegar, parsley and pepper to taste, blending well. Serve at once while still hot, garnished with parsley sprigs.

SERVES 4-6

Nutritional content per serving: Carbohydrate: 20 g Fat: 19 g Fibre: 10 g Kilocalories: 285

MAIN COURSE SALADS

TIP THE BALANCE IN YOUR FAVOUR; FORGET THE MYTH OF SALADS BEING SO-CALLED 'RABBIT' FOOD AND DELVE INTO THIS MOUTH-WATERING SELECTION OF MAIN COURSE OFFERINGS. ALWAYS SUBSTANTIAL, AND OFTEN HEARTY, THEY OFFER A GOOD HEALTHY ALTERNATIVE TO HOT MAIN COURSE MEALS.

Rosy duck salad

VARY THE CITRUS FRUITS IN THIS SALAD ACCORDING TO SEASON – REPLACE THE ORANGES AND GRAPEFRUIT WITH MINNEOLAS, KUMQUATS, TANGERINES OR SATSUMAS, WHEN AVAILABLE IN THE SHOPS

2.5 kg (5 lb) oven-ready duckling
2 blood oranges, peeled, pith removed and segmented
50 g (2 oz) walnut pieces
1 quantity Spiced Orange Mayonnaise (see page 92)
1 radicchio, separated into leaves
1 small red pepper, cored, deseeded and sliced
1 small yellow pepper, cored, deseeded and sliced
about 8-12 cherry tomatoes, halved if large
1 pink grapefruit, peeled, pith removed and segmented
salt

Wash and dry the duckling and prick the flesh with a fork. Rub the skin with salt and place on a rack or trivet in a roasting tin. Roast in a preheated oven, 180°C, 350°F, Gas Mark 4, for 2½-3 hours. Allow to cool completely.

Strip off the duckling skin and crisp it under a preheated hot grill, then allow to cool. Remove the meat from the duckling and cut into bite-sized pieces. Mix with the oranges, walnuts and mayonnaise.

Pile the duck mixture on to a serving dish and surround with a decorative border of radicchio, peppers, tomatoes and pink grapefruit. Scatter over the crisp duckling skin and serve as soon as possible.

SERVES 4-6

Nutritional content per serving: Carbohydrate: 14 g Fat: 47 g Fibre: 3 g Kilocalories: 671

Crunchy turkey and fruit salad

THIS COLOURFUL, CRISP SALAD HAS A LOW-CALORIE YOGURT DRESSING WHICH MAKES IT PERFECT FOR THOSE ON A SLIMMING DIET. IT PROVIDES JUST 176 KILOCALORIES PER PORTION AND TASTES DELICIOUS

250 g (8 oz) cooked turkey, sliced
175 g (6 oz) fresh bean sprouts
75 g (3 oz) seedless white grapes
75 g (3 oz) black grapes, halved and deseeded
250 g (8 oz) strawberries, halved or sliced
1 round lettuce, separated into leaves
DRESSING:
150 g (5.3 oz) carton low-fat natural yogurt
2 teaspoons white wine vinegar
1 teaspoon lemon juice
dash of soy sauce
salt and pepper

Place the turkey, bean sprouts, grapes and strawberries in a bowl and toss lightly to mix.

Arrange the lettuce on a large serving plate and pile the turkey mixture on top.

To make the dressing, mix the yogurt with the vinegar, lemon juice, soy sauce and salt and pepper to taste. Spoon the dressing over the salad to serve.

SERVES 4

Nutritional content per serving: Carbohydrate: 15 g Fat: 2 g Fibre: 2 g Kilocalories: 176

Rosy Duck Salad; Crunchy Turkey and Fruit Salad

Tuna Salad

Over the years I have made this salad more times than I care to remember but no one seems to mind – least of all me since, if made with canned beans and sweetcorn, it's one of the speediest main meal salad combinations I know. This salad is suitable for freezing in a sealed container for up to 3 months without the dressing

50 g (2 oz) long-grain rice
125 g (4 oz) cooked kidney beans
125 g (4 oz) sweetcorn
200 g (7 oz) can tuna in oil or brine, drained and flaked
1 small green pepper, cored, deseeded and sliced
5 tablespoons Chiffonade Dressing (see page 92) or French Dressing (see page 85)
1 tablespoon chopped parsley
salt
parsley sprigs to garnish

Cook the rice in boiling salted water, according to the packet instructions, until tender. Drain thoroughly and allow to cool.

Place the rice in a large bowl with the kidney beans, sweetcorn, flaked tuna and green pepper. Add the dressing and parsley and toss gently to coat and mix. Serve garnished with parsley sprigs.

SERVES 4

Nutritional content per serving: Carbohydrate: 21 g Fat: 21 g Fibre: 5 g Kilocalories: 341

Egg and Avocado Salad à la Grecque

Hard-boiled eggs make a tasty and nourishing storecupboard standby ingredient for all salad meals. Serve this egg salad with different types of bread, warmed and cut in chunks

8 hard-boiled eggs
3 ripe avocados, peeled and stoned
1 small crisp lettuce, torn into pieces
12 black olives
56 g (2 oz) can anchovy fillets, rinsed, dried and halved
2 tablespoons chopped parsley
DRESSING:
5 tablespoons olive oil
2 tablespoons lemon juice
2 teaspoons Dijon mustard
1 teaspoon clear honey
salt and pepper

Make the dressing first; beat the oil with the lemon juice, mustard, honey and salt and pepper to taste until well blended.

Shell the eggs and cut into wedges or slices. Slice the avocados into thick pieces and place in a bowl with the eggs. Pour over half of the dressing and toss lightly to mix and coat.

Place the lettuce in a serving dish and arrange the egg and avocado mixture on top. Scatter over the olives and anchovy fillets. Pour over the remaining salad dressing and sprinkle with parsley to serve.

SERVES 4

Nutritional content per serving: Carbohydrate: 5 g Fat: 68 g Fibre: 4 g Kilocalories: 732

Tuna Salad; Chef's Salad; Egg and Avocado Salad à la Grecque

CHEF'S SALAD

THERE DOESN'T SEEM TO BE ANY FIXED INGREDIENT IN A CHEF'S SALAD – IT'S SIMPLY A CLEVER WAY OF COMBINING A NUMBER OF COMPATIBLE FOODS (PERHAPS WITH LEFTOVERS) FOR A TASTY MAIN MEAL DISH

½ Cos lettuce, torn into pieces
1 bunch radishes, sliced
¼ cucumber, sliced thinly
1 small red onion, sliced into rings
250 g (8 oz) cooked gammon
125 g (4 oz) Danish Blue cheese
6 tablespoons French Dressing (see page 85)

Place the lettuce, radishes, cucumber and onion in layers in a serving bowl.

Cut the gammon into fairly thick strips and add to the salad bowl. Dice the cheese into small cubes and scatter over the gammon.

Just before serving, pour the dressing over the salad. Toss gently to coat and mix if liked, or serve still arranged in layers.

SERVES 4

Nutritional content per serving: Carbohydrate: 2 g Fat: 29 g Fibre: 1 g Kilocalories: 380

MEDITERRANEAN SALAD

THIS HEARTY, COLOURFUL MAIN MEAL SALAD OF TUNA WITH MEDITERRANEAN-STYLE VEGETABLES SHOULD BE SERVED WITH HOT, CRUSTY FRENCH BREAD FOR MOPPING UP ANY LEFTOVER HERBY DRESSING

1 clove garlic, cut in half
1 lettuce heart, cut into wedges
4 tomatoes, cut into wedges
8 black olives
1 small onion, sliced into rings
1 yellow pepper, cored, deseeded and sliced
200 g (7 oz) can tuna in oil
125 g (4 oz) dwarf green beans
about 2 tablespoons olive oil
1 tablespoon red wine vinegar
2 tablespoons chopped mixed herbs (for example, parsley, chives and basil)
salt and pepper

Rub a serving bowl with the cut clove of garlic. Add the lettuce heart, tomatoes, olives, onion and yellow pepper. Drain the oil from the tuna and reserve. Flake the fish into bite-sized pieces and add to the salad mixture.

Cook the beans in boiling salted water until tender but still crisp, about 3 minutes. Drain and refresh under cold running water. Drain again thoroughly, then add to the tuna mixture.

To make the dressing, make the tuna oil up to 4 tablespoons with the olive oil. Beat with the vinegar, herbs and salt and pepper to taste until well blended. Spoon over the salad and toss gently to mix and coat. Serve at once.

SERVES 4

Nutritional content per serving: Carbohydrate: 4 g Fat: 18 g Fibre: 3 g Kilocalories: 228

PARADISI CHICKEN SALAD

A FRESH-TASTING COMBINATION OF STRIPS OF CHICKEN AND SEGMENTS OF SUMMER GRAPEFRUIT, THIS SALAD IS ALSO KNOWN AS CITRUS PARADISI (PARADISI MEANING GRAPEFRUIT IN LATIN). IT CAN BE SERVED WITH PLAIN OR GARLIC-FLAVOURED CROÛTONS

1 round lettuce, torn into pieces
about 50 g (2 oz) frisée or escarole, torn into pieces
about 50 g (2 oz) lamb's lettuce, separated into leaves
¼ cucumber, sliced
2 grapefruit, peeled, pith removed and segmented
375 g (12 oz) cooked chicken, cut into strips
1 green or yellow pepper, cored, deseeded and sliced
plain or garlic-flavoured croûtons (see page 95)
DRESSING:
225 g (7 oz) carton Greek yogurt
2-3 tablespoons fresh grapefruit juice
salt and pepper

Place the lettuce, frisée, lamb's lettuce and cucumber in a bowl and toss lightly together. Add the grapefruit to the lettuce mixture with the chicken and sliced pepper. Cover and chill for 30 minutes.

To make the dressing, mix the yogurt with the grapefruit juice and salt and pepper to taste.

To serve, divide the chicken salad evenly between four individual serving plates. Scatter with a few croûtons. Drizzle over the prepared dressing and serve at once.

SERVES 4

Nutritional content per serving: Carbohydrate: 10 g Fat: 6 g Fibre: 2 g Kilocalories: 206

Paradisi Chicken Salad; Mediterranean Salad; Minted Lamb Salad

MINTED LAMB SALAD

AN ELEGANT LAMB SALAD WITH A TASTY DRESSING THAT MAKES A REFRESHINGLY LIGHT SUMMER MEAL

250 g (8 oz) cucumber, sliced
2 large ripe pears, peeled, cored and sliced
1 red pepper, cored, deseeded and sliced
1 bunch spring onions, chopped
375 g (12 oz) cold roast lamb
mint sprigs to garnish
DRESSING:
150 g (5.3 oz) carton natural yogurt
3 tablespoons mint jelly
salt and pepper

Mix the cucumber slices with the sliced pears, red pepper and spring onions.

To make the dressing, mix the yogurt with the mint jelly and salt and pepper to taste, blending well. Pour over the pear mixture and toss gently to coat and mix. Spoon on to a large serving plate.

Slice the cold roast lamb into thin julienne strips and place on top of the salad mixture. Garnish with mint sprigs to serve.

SERVES 4

Nutritional content per serving: Carbohydrate: 26 g Fat: 8 g Fibre: 3 g Kilocalories: 311

LINCOLNSHIRE DUCK SALAD

CRISPY, SUCCULENT AND MOUTH-WATERING DUCKLING IS DELICIOUS SERVED COLD IN A SALAD FOR SUMMER-TIME OUTDOOR EATING. ACCOMPANY WITH A FULL-FLAVOURED WHITE WINE FOR A MEMORABLE MEAL

2.5 kg (5 lb) oven-ready duckling
5 large oranges, peeled, pith removed and segmented
5 sticks celery, chopped
1 Cos lettuce, torn into pieces
1-2 bunches watercress
DRESSING:
6 tablespoons safflower oil
2 tablespoons white wine vinegar
1 tablespoon clear honey
1 tablespoon finely chopped onion or shallot
½ clove garlic, chopped finely
pinch of mustard powder
salt and pepper

Wash and dry the duckling and prick the flesh with a fork. Rub the skin with salt and place on a rack or trivet in a roasting tin. Roast in a preheated oven, 180°C, 350°F, Gas Mark 4, for 2½-3 hours. Allow to cool completely.

Remove the meat from the duckling and cut into bite-sized pieces. Mix it with 4 of the oranges, the celery and lettuce.

To make the dressing, beat the oil with the vinegar, honey, onion or shallot, garlic, mustard and salt and pepper to taste until well blended. Pour over the salad just before serving and toss gently to coat and mix. Garnish with the watercress and remaining orange segments.

Microwave: Place the duckling, breast-side down, on a roasting rack in a dish and microwave on Full Power for 10 minutes. Turn breast-side up, drain away excess fat and microwave for a further 15 minutes. Drain again and microwave for a further 10-15 minutes. Leave to stand, covered with foil, until cold. Remove the flesh and cut into bite-sized pieces. Mix the duck with 4 of the segmented oranges, the celery and lettuce. Pour over the dressing just before serving and toss to coat and mix. Serve garnished with the watercress and remaining orange segments.

SERVES 6

Nutritional content per serving: Carbohydrate: 14 g Fat: 29 g Fibre: 5 g Kilocalories: 470

SEAFOOD SALAD

ALMOST ANY COMBINATION OF FRESHLY COOKED SEAFOOD MAY BE USED IN THIS SALAD – CHOOSE FROM PRAWNS, SHRIMPS, MUSSELS, SCALLOPS, LOBSTER OR CRAB. THE GRATED LEMON RIND, HOWEVER, IS A MUST!

750 g (1½ lb) cooked shelled shellfish (see above)
¼ cucumber, sliced thinly
2 sticks celery, chopped
1 tablespoon grated lemon rind
6 tablespoons Thousand Island Dressing (see page 89) or Normandy Dressing (see page 91)
2 lemons, sliced thinly
dill sprigs to garnish

Cut the shellfish into bite-sized pieces if large. Place in a bowl with the cucumber, celery and lemon rind. Add the dressing and toss lightly to mix and coat.

Chill lightly before spooning on to a serving dish. Surround with slices of lemon and garnish with dill sprigs.

SERVES 4

Nutritional content per serving: Carbohydrate: 2 g Fat: 21 g Fibre: 1 g Kilocalories: 351

Turkey and Walnut Rice Salad; Seafood Salad; Lincolnshire Duck Salad

TURKEY AND WALNUT RICE SALAD

THE TIME-SAVING MANDARIN YOGURT DRESSING FOR THIS NOURISHING, FRUITY SALAD CAN BE MADE WITH NATURAL YOGURT INSTEAD; IN THAT CASE, ADD 1 TEASPOON GRATED ORANGE OR OTHER CITRUS FRUIT RIND WITH SEASONING TO TASTE

125 g (4 oz) long-grain rice
375 g (12 oz) cooked turkey
2 red dessert apples, cored and chopped
2 teaspoons lemon juice
4 sticks celery, chopped
40 g (1½ oz) walnuts, chopped
4 tablespoons mandarin yogurt
½ teaspoon caraway seeds
lettuce leaves to serve
salt and pepper

Cook the rice in boiling salted water, according to the packet instructions, until tender. Drain thoroughly and allow to cool.

Chop the turkey into bite-sized pieces and place in a bowl with the cooked rice. Toss the apple pieces in the lemon juice and add to the turkey mixture with the celery and walnuts.

Mix the yogurt with half of the caraway seeds and salt and pepper to taste. Fold into the turkey mixture.

Line 4 individual plates with lettuce leaves and pile the turkey mixture on top. Sprinkle with the remaining caraway seeds to serve.

SERVES 4

Nutritional content per serving: Carbohydrate: 38 g Fat: 8 g Fibre: 4 g Kilocalories: 345

Parma Ham, Fig and Mint Salad

Ever since my fig trees came into fruit some 5 years ago, I have been trying out recipes that do justice to the figs' subtle pink flesh and reward me for the regular watering, pruning and general care I have lavished upon them. This recipe does both. It is a light main meal, just the thing for the typical appetite-suppressing weather of the late summer months

feuille de chêne or quattro stagione leaves to serve
about 1 kg (2 lb) fresh figs
125 g (4 oz) Parma ham
mint sprigs to garnish
DRESSING:
3 large mint sprigs
3 tablespoons lemon juice
150 ml (5 fl oz) carton soured cream
1 teaspoon snipped chives
salt and pepper

Arrange the feuille de chêne leaves on a serving plate. Carefully peel the figs, then make a cross from the top of each almost to the base with a sharp knife and carefully ease apart into petal shapes. Place on the serving plate.

Cut the Parma ham into strips and arrange around the prepared figs. Cover and chill until required.

To make the dressing, strip the leaves from the mint and place in a bowl with the lemon juice. Crush lightly with a fork and leave for at least 10 minutes for the mint to flavour the juice. Strain well, discarding the mint leaves, and season with a little salt and pepper. Stir into the soured cream with the chives, blending well.

To serve, spoon the dressing over the ham and figs. Garnish with mint sprigs and serve immediately.

SERVES 4

Nutritional content per serving: Carbohydrate: 25 g Fat: 15 g Fibre: 7 g Kilocalories: 283

Parma Ham, Fig and Mint Salad

Bacchanalian Beef and Fruit Salad

BACCHANALIAN BEEF AND FRUIT SALAD

BACCHUS, THE GREEK GOD OF WINE, WOULD SURELY APPROVE OF THIS PLEASURABLE TENDER BEEF AND LIQUEUR-SOAKED FRUIT SALAD. THE COOKED RICE MAY BE REPLACED WITH A RICE AND GRAIN MIXTURE OR JUST CHOPPED NUTS

2 ripe paw-paw
75 g (3 oz) black grapes, halved and deseeded
40 g (1½ oz) dried apricots, cut into strips
50 g (2 oz) cooked white long-grain rice
2 tablespoons lemon juice
2 tablespoons Cointreau or Orange Curaçao liqueur
1 pink grapefruit, peeled, pith removed and diced
3 tablespoons redcurrant or cranberry jelly
1 teaspoon horseradish relish
4 small lettuce heart leaves
375 g (12 oz) roast beef, sliced thinly
salt and pepper
dill sprigs to garnish

Halve the paw-paw, remove the seeds and flesh and cut the latter into small cubes, keeping the skins intact. Place in a bowl with the grapes, apricots, rice, lemon juice, liqueur and salt and pepper to taste. Mix, then spoon back into the paw-paw, cover and leave to stand while preparing the remaining salad ingredients.

Mix the grapefruit with the redcurrant jelly and horseradish, blending well. Spoon on to the lettuce heart leaves.

To serve, arrange the beef on a flat serving dish with the fruit salad shells and pickle-filled lettuce leaves. Garnish with dill sprigs and serve as soon as possible.

SERVES 4

Nutritional content per serving: Carbohydrate: 35 g Fat: 5 g Fibre: 3 g Kilocalories: 308

SICILIAN SEAFOOD SALAD

IT IS OFTEN SAID THAT GOOD THINGS COST ONE DEAR AND IT IS TRUE THAT THIS RECIPE, WHICH USES THE VERY BEST OF FRESH SEAFOOD, IS PERHAPS NOT AN EVERDAY MAIN MEAL SALAD. SAVE IT FOR SPECIAL CELEBRATORY OCCASIONS, WHEN ITS IMPACT ON THE POCKET MIGHT NOT SEEM TOO HARSH. TOSS IN A LIGHT VINAIGRETTE OR CREAMY THOUSAND ISLAND DRESSING

150 ml (¼ pint) dry white wine
150 ml (¼ pint) water
4 tablespoons lemon juice
2 shallots or 1 small onion, chopped finely
1 tablespoon chopped parsley
½ clove garlic, crushed
about 750 g (1½ lb) prepared fresh seafood (such as scrubbed mussels in shells, prepared squid and raw or cooked prawns or langoustine)
6 tablespoons Classic Vinaigrette (see page 85) or Thousand Island Dressing (see page 89)
1 feuille de chêne or quattro stagione, separated into leaves
lemon slices or wedges to garnish

Place the wine, water, lemon juice, shallots or onion, parsley and garlic in a large pan. Bring to the boil, add the chosen prepared seafood in batches, and boil, according to type, until cooked. (The cooking time may be as little as 2-3 minutes for raw prawns and up to 15 minutes for large squid.) Remove when cooked with a slotted spoon and place in a bowl before starting the next batch. Finally pour the cooking liquor over the seafood mixture, cover and chill until cold.

Drain the liquor from the cooked seafood. Add the classic vinaigrette or thousand island dressing to the seafood and toss lightly to coat and mix.

Place the feuille de chêne leaves on individual serving dishes and then add the seafood mixture. Garnish with lemon slices or wedges and serve as soon as possible.

SERVES 4-6

Nutritional content per serving: Carbohydrate: 2 g Fat: 30 g Fibre: 2 g Kilocalories: 394

TARRAGON AND THYME CHICKEN SALAD

THIS DELICIOUSLY SIMPLE CHICKEN SALAD RECIPE USES ONE OF THE TASTY HERB MUSTARDS. IF YOU CANNOT BUY TARRAGON AND THYME MUSTARD, THEN ADD A LITTLE CHOPPED FRESH TARRAGON AND THYME TO YOUR FAVOURITE MUSTARD. SERVE WITH COLD COOKED RICE

2 kg (4 lb) chicken, roasted
4 sticks celery, chopped
1 red dessert apple, cored and sliced
1 green pepper, cored, deseeded and sliced
½ round lettuce, separated into leaves
25 g (1 oz) slivered almonds, toasted
thyme sprigs to garnish
DRESSING:
4 tablespoons Mayonnaise (see page 7)
4 tablespoons soured cream
2 tablespoons tarragon and thyme mustard
salt and pepper

Remove the skin from the cold roast chicken and chop the meat into bite-sized pieces. Place in a bowl with the celery, apple and green pepper.

To make the dressing, mix the mayonnaise with the soured cream, mustard and salt and pepper to taste. Fold into the chicken mixture to coat evenly.

Line individual serving plates with the lettuce leaves and top with the chicken mixture. Sprinkle with the toasted almonds and garnish with thyme sprigs. Serve lightly chilled.

SERVES 4-6

Nutritional content per serving: Carbohydrate: 6 g Fat: 31 g Fibre: 4 g Kilocalories: 495

Sicilian Seafood Salad; Tarragon and Thyme Chicken Salad

PASTA SALAD BLUES

THIS RICH, SATISFYING CHEESE AND PASTA SALAD CAN ALSO BE MADE USING ONE OF THE LUXURY BLUE CHEESES LIKE MYCELLA, GORGONZOLA, DOLCELATTE OR RIPE BLUE STILTON

250 g (8 oz) pasta shells
1 teaspoon vegetable oil
50 g (2 oz) cooked peas
50 g (2 oz) cooked carrots, diced
25 g (1 oz) Danish Blue cheese
250 g (8 oz) cooked ham, sliced or cubed
salt and pepper
watercress to garnish
DRESSING:
75 g (3 oz) Danish Blue cheese
3 tablespoons Mayonnaise (see page 7)
2 teaspoons lemon juice

Cook the pasta shells in boiling salted water with the oil, according to the packet instructions, until *al dente*. Drain and cool under cold water. Drain again thoroughly.

Mix the cooked pasta with the peas and carrots. Cut the cheese into cubes and reserve.

To make the dressing, mash the cheese with the mayonnaise, lemon juice and pepper to taste. Fold half of the dressing into the pasta mixture and place on a serving dish. Top with the ham and reserved cubed cheese. Garnish with the watercress. Serve the remaining dressing separately.

SERVES 4

Nutritional content per serving: Carbohydrate: 51 g Fat: 22 g Fibre: 2 g Kilocalories: 495

Pasta Salad Blues

Tongue, Red Cabbage and Apple Salad

TONGUE, RED CABBAGE AND APPLE SALAD

THIS IS A SPLENDID RECIPE FOR THE WINTER MONTHS – I OFTEN MAKE IT AFTER CHRISTMAS TO USE UP THE REMAINS OF A COOKED TONGUE, FESTIVE PICKLED RED CABBAGE AND COX'S APPLES. IT IS DELICIOUS SERVED WITH THIN FINGERS OF PUMPERNICKEL BREAD SPREAD WITH A LITTLE BUTTER OR FULL-FAT SOFT CHEESE

- 125 g (4 oz) spring greens or ½ head Chinese leaves
- 4 tablespoons Honey Dressing (see page 86) or Port Dressing (see page 92)
- 250 g (8 oz) boiled potatoes
- 250 g (8 oz) cooked tongue
- 75 g (3 oz) pickled red cabbage
- 1 stick celery, chopped
- 1 large Cox's apple, cored and chopped
- 2 tablespoons chopped parsley

Remove any stalks from the spring greens or Chinese leaves, then shred very finely. Toss in 2 tablespoons of the dressing, then use to line the outer edge of a large shallow serving plate.

Slice the potatoes into rounds and cut the tongue into thin strips. Place in a bowl with the pickled red cabbage, celery, apple, parsley and remaining dressing. Toss gently to coat and mix. Spoon into the centre of the dish and serve as soon as possible.

SERVES 4

Nutritional content per serving: Carbohydrate: 20 g Fat: 15 g Fibre: 4 g Kilocalories: 265

RUSTIC BEEF SALAD

THIS IS A GREAT WAY TO FINISH THE REMAINS OF A SUNDAY BEEF ROAST. THE PICKLES CAN BE VARIED: TRY PICKLED CUCUMBERS, CARROTS, CABBAGE, ONIONS AND CAULIFLOWER, FOR EXAMPLE. SERVE AT ROOM TEMPERATURE WITH LOTS OF WARM CRUSTY BREAD

500 g (1 lb) cold cooked roast or spiced beef
125 g (4 oz) button mushrooms, quartered
1 crisp red dessert apple, peeled, cored and sliced thinly
about 125 g (4 oz) pickles, sliced if large
½ small red pepper, cored, deseeded and sliced
1 red onion, sliced into rings
1 tablespoon chopped parsley
feuille de chêne or quattro stagione leaves to serve
DRESSING:
4 tablespoons sunflower or walnut oil
2 tablespoons red wine vinegar
½ teaspoon Worcestershire sauce
½ teaspoon caraway seeds (optional)
salt and pepper

Cut the beef into thin bite-sized strips and place in a large bowl. Add the mushrooms, apple, pickles, red pepper, onion rings and parsley.

To make the dressing, beat the oil and the vinegar with the Worcestershire sauce, caraway seeds, if using, and salt and pepper to taste. Pour over the salad and toss gently to mix and coat. Cover and leave to stand for at least 15 minutes for the flavours to develop.

Toss the salad again lightly before serving on plates lined with feuille de chêne or quattro stagione leaves.

SERVES 4

Nutritional content per serving: Carbohydrate: 7 g Fat: 21 g Fibre: 3 g Kilocalories: 378

MR MCGREGOR'S SALAD

I FIRST MADE THIS SALAD AT A FRIEND'S COTTAGE RETREAT DEEP IN THE COUNTRY. I FELT PRIVILEGED TO REACH THE WILD SALAD INGREDIENTS – PURSLANE, DANDELION, BURNET AND WILD CHICORY – BEFORE THE RABBITS! YOU CAN, HOWEVER, MAKE THE SALAD WITH THE EASIER-TO-FIND RED CHICORY, FRISEE AND LAMB'S LETTUCE. YOU CAN ALSO SUBSTITUTE 1 HEN'S EGG FOR 3 QUAIL'S EGGS

about 375 g (12 oz) mixed fresh or wild salad leaves (such as frisée or escarole, wild or red chicory, lamb's lettuce, purslane, dandelion and burnet)
a large handful of garlic croûtons (see page 95)
12 quail's eggs
175 g (6 oz) smoked bacon, derinded and chopped
3 tablespoons white wine vinegar
salt and pepper
1 tablespoon snipped chives to garnish

Line 4 individual serving plates with the salad leaves and scatter over the croûtons.

Gently break the eggs into boiling water with a little vinegar and poach – they will be ready in about 1 minute. Remove with a slotted spoon and place 3 on top of each serving.

Fry the bacon gently in a frying pan without any additional fat until crisp and all the fat has been released. Remove with a slotted spoon and scatter over the salad plates evenly.

To make the dressing, stir the vinegar into the hot bacon fat, blending well. Season with salt and pepper and spoon over the salads. Sprinkle with chives and serve at once.

SERVES 4

Nutritional content per serving: Carbohydrate: 5 g Fat: 27 g Fibre: 2 g Kilocalories: 335

Rustic Beef Salad; Mr McGregor's Salad

Deli Special

I HAVE MADE VARIATIONS OF THIS SALAD MANY, MANY TIMES. I CHOOSE THE MEATS AND CHEESE LITERALLY AT THE DELICATESSEN COUNTER, AFTER CHECKING WHAT IS ON OFFER, WHAT LOOKS ESPECIALLY GOOD AND SUITS THE TASTE OF THE PEOPLE TO WHOM I INTEND TO SERVE IT. PLENTY OF WARM CRUSTY BREAD IS THE PERFECT ACCOMPANIMENT

500 g (1 lb) minced cooked deli meats (such as German wursts, salami, pastrami, salt beef, smoked ham), sliced
250 g (8 oz) smoked cheese, diced
1 green pepper, cored, deseeded and chopped
1 red pepper, cored, deseeded and chopped
2 small pickled gherkins, sliced thinly
4 tablespoons Classic Vinaigrette (see page 85)
2 spring onions, shredded finely

Arrange the sliced deli meats around the edge of a large serving plate. Mix the diced cheese with the peppers and gherkins and spoon into the centre of the meats.

Just before serving, spoon or drizzle the dressing over the meat and cheese mixture. Scatter over the spring onions and serve at once.

SERVES 4-6

Nutritional content per serving: Carbohydrate: 2 g Fat: 50 g Fibre: 1 g Kilocalories: 633

Hollywood 'Artist's' Salad

NANETTE NEWMAN FIRST DESCRIBED THIS SALAD LUNCH IDEA TO ME – IT IS A SPECIALITY OF THE BEVERLY HILLS HOTEL. I AM UNLIKELY IN THE NEAR FUTURE TO TASTE THIS FOOD LOVER'S DISH FIRST-HAND, SO THIS IS MY INTERPRETATION OF WHAT SEEMS LIKE AN ARTIST'S PALETTE OF DELICIOUS FRESH SALAD INGREDIENTS WITH FULL-FAT COTTAGE OR SOFT CHEESE

1 small to medium watermelon
375 g (12 oz) full-fat cottage or full-fat soft cheese
1 tablespoon snipped chives
50 g (2 oz) fresh pineapple, chopped finely
about 1 kg (2 lb) fresh fruits (the very best in season such as strawberries, nectarines, kiwi fruit, raspberries, cherries, grapes, figs and lychees)
salt and pepper
4-6 spring onions (optional)

Cut the watermelon into slices about 1-2 cm (½-¾ inch) thick, rather like large plates. (The number of slices will depend upon the size of the watermelon but usually it will cut into 4-6 slices.) Place on large individual serving plates.

Mix the chosen cheese with the chives, pineapple and salt and pepper to taste. Place a small mound on each watermelon slice.

Prepare the fruits according to type and arrange attractively on the watermelon slices – ideally group portions of fruit on the melon rather like the colours on an artist's palette.

Finish each serving with a small edible 'paintbrush', made by thinly slicing the end of a spring onion to resemble a paintbrush head. Place at an angle on the salad to serve.

SERVES 4-6

Nutritional content per serving: Carbohydrate: 40 g Fat: 4 g Fibre: 9 g Kilocalories: 249

Deli Special; Hollywood 'Artist's' Salad; Puzzled Trout and Kiwi Salad

PUZZLED TROUT AND KIWI SALAD

FRIENDS WERE DELIGHTED WITH THE COMBINATION OF FLAVOURS THIS SALAD HAD TO OFFER. MIXING AND MATCHING THE CLEAN TASTES OF RASPBERRY VINEGAR, KIWI FRUIT AND GRAPESEED OIL WITH THE SMOKEY FLAVOUR OF TROUT PROVED A WINNER

250 g (8 oz) pasta bows
1 teaspoon vegetable oil
375 g (12 oz) smoked trout, skinned, boned and flaked
2 kiwi fruit, peeled and sliced thinly
250 g (8 oz) cherry tomatoes
2 tablespoons chopped parsley
DRESSING:
2 tablespoons grapeseed oil
3 tablespoons raspberry vinegar
1 teaspoon wholegrain mustard (Moutarde de Meaux)
salt and pepper

Cook the pasta bows in boiling salted water with the vegetable oil, according to the packet instructions, until *al dente*.

Meanwhile, to make the dressing, beat the grapeseed oil with the vinegar, mustard and salt and pepper to taste until well blended.

Drain the pasta thoroughly then, while still hot, add the dressing and toss gently to coat. Allow to cool.

Add the trout, kiwi fruit, cherry tomatoes and parsley and toss gently to mix. Serve at room temperature as soon as possible.

SERVES 4

Nutritional content per serving: Carbohydrate: 52 g Fat: 13 g Fibre: 2 g Kilocalories: 443

Classic Salads

EVERY COUNTRY'S CUISINE HAS ITS CLASSIC SALAD REPERTOIRE USING THE BEST OF LOCAL VEGETABLES, FRUITS, NUTS, OILS, VINEGARS, SPICES AND HERBS. THIS SELECTION, THOUGH BY NO MEANS COMPLETE, DOES SPAN THE GLOBE, COVERING RUSSIA, FRANCE, AMERICA, SWITZERLAND, SPAIN, BRITAIN, HUNGARY . . .

CAESAR'S SALAD

THE DRESSING FOR A CLASSIC CAESAR'S SALAD IS MADE WITH EGGS THAT HAVE BEEN PAR-BOILED FOR 1 MINUTE ONLY – THIS HELPS TO PRODUCE A VELVETY-SMOOTH COATING FOR THE LETTUCE, ANCHOVIES AND PARMESAN CHEESE

2 tablespoons olive oil
1 clove garlic, crushed
2 tablespoons lemon juice
50 g (2 oz) can anchovies in oil
2 eggs
1 large Cos lettuce, separated into leaves
3 quantities garlic croûtons (see page 95)
4 tablespoons grated fresh Parmesan cheese
salt and pepper

Mix the oil with the garlic (and if there is time leave to stand for 30 minutes for the flavours to develop).

Add the lemon juice to the garlic-flavoured oil with salt and pepper to taste. Drain the oil from the anchovies and add it to the lemon juice mixture. Chop the anchovies into small pieces and add to the dressing.

Par-boil the eggs in boiling water for 1 minute, then shell and add to the dressing; beat well to incorporate the partially set white.

Place the lettuce leaves in a bowl, tearing any larger leaves into pieces. Add the dressing and toss well to coat. Scatter over the croûtons and Parmesan cheese and toss again to mix. Serve at once.

SERVES 6

Nutritional content per serving: Carbohydrate: 7 g Fat: 22 g Fibre: 2 g Kilocalories: 267

WALDORF SALAD

EVERYONE SEEMS TO HAVE A FAVOURITE WALDORF SALAD RECIPE AND THIS IS MINE. OCCASIONALLY I VARY THE INGREDIENTS AND USE A MIXTURE OF PEAR SLICES AND PINEAPPLE CHUNKS INSTEAD OF DESSERT APPLES

4 sticks celery, chopped
3 red dessert apples, cored and sliced
25 g (1 oz) walnut pieces
salt and pepper
parsley sprigs to garnish
DRESSING:
½ quantity Mayonnaise (see page 7)
2 tablespoons natural yogurt
1 tablespoon chopped parsley

To make the dressing, mix the mayonnaise with the yogurt and salt and pepper to taste.

Add the celery, apples and walnut pieces and toss together to coat and mix. Spoon into a shallow serving dish and sprinkle with the chopped parsley. Garnish with parsley sprigs.

SERVES 4-6

Nutritional content per serving: Carbohydrate: 11 g Fat: 43 g Fibre: 3 g Kilocalories: 442

Caesar's Salad; Waldorf Salad

Spinach and Bacon Salad

THE SECRET OF THIS FAVOURITE SALAD IS TO SERVE IT WHILE THE DRESSING IS STILL WARM AND THE SALAD LEAVES STILL LOOK AND TASTE FRESH BUT ARE JUST STARTING TO WILT

500 g (1 lb) young spinach leaves
1 small bunch spring onions, shredded into julienne strips
2 tablespoons sunflower oil
1 clove garlic, crushed
4 rashers unsmoked or smoked back bacon, derinded and chopped
2 tablespoons red wine vinegar
1 egg, beaten
pinch of brown sugar
pepper

Make sure the spinach leaves are thoroughly rinsed and dry, then tear and place in a serving bowl with the spring onions.

Mix the oil with the garlic and leave to stand as long as possible before straining.

Fry the bacon in a frying pan without any additional fat until crisp, brown and all the bacon fat has been released. Remove with a slotted spoon, drain on kitchen paper, then scatter over the spinach mixture.

Meanwhile, beat the vinegar with the egg, sugar and pepper to taste and stir into the hot bacon fat with the strained garlic oil. Mix well for a few seconds to allow the dressing to thicken slightly, then spoon over the salad, toss gently to coat and mix, and serve at once.

SERVES 4-6

Nutritional content per serving: Carbohydrate: 8 g Fat: 20 g Fibre: 1 g Kilocalories: 241

Salade Niçoise

I NEVER TIRE OF THIS CLASSIC SALAD AND OFTEN SERVE IT TO FRIENDS FOR LUNCH. WITH A BOTTLE OF DRY WHITE WINE AND WARMED, CRUSTY FRENCH BREAD, WHAT COULD BE MORE DELICIOUS?

4 medium potatoes, scrubbed
250 g (8 oz) dwarf green beans
4 tomatoes, skinned and cut into wedges
200 g (7 oz) can tuna in oil
about 3 tablespoons sunflower oil
2 tablespoons white wine vinegar
¼ teaspoon mustard
50 g (2 oz) can anchovies in oil, drained
about 12 black olives
1 tablespoon capers
1 small crisp lettuce, separated into leaves
salt and pepper

Boil or steam the potatoes in their skins, in or over boiling salted water until tender, about 15-20 minutes, depending upon size. Drain thoroughly and allow to cool.

Cook the beans in boiling salted water until tender, about 6-8 minutes. Drain thoroughly and allow to cool.

Cut the potatoes into bite-sized cubes and the beans into 2.5 cm (1 inch) lengths. Mix the potatoes with the beans and tomatoes.

Drain the oil from the tuna into a bowl and make up to 5 tablespoons with the sunflower oil. Beat in the wine vinegar, mustard and salt and pepper to taste.

Flake the tuna and add to the potato mixture with the anchovies, black olives and capers. Pour over the dressing and toss gently to coat and mix.

Line a serving dish with the lettuce leaves and spoon the salad mixture on top. Serve as soon as possible.

SERVES 4

Nutritional content per serving: Carbohydrate: 28 g Fat: 27 g Fibre: 8 g Kilocalories: 427

Spinach and Bacon Salad; Hungarian Tomato Salad; Salad Niçoise

HUNGARIAN TOMATO SALAD

THIS SIDE OR APPETIZER SALAD SHOULD BE MADE WITH CHERRY TOMATOES, AND TOPPED WITH A CREAMY HORSERADISH DRESSING. IT IS DELICIOUS WITH COLD ROAST OR SPICED BEEF. WHEN AVOCADOS ARE CHEAP AND PLENTIFUL THEY CAN BE LACED WITH LEMON AND PARSLEY AND USED IN PLACE OF THE HORSERADISH TO MAKE A DRESSING

500 g (1 lb) cherry tomatoes, skinned
4 tablespoons Mayonnaise (see page 7)
1 tablespoon creamed horseradish
1 tablespoon lemon juice
3 tablespoons double cream or soured cream
salt and pepper
1 tablespoon snipped chives
1 teaspoon paprika
chives to garnish

Pile the tomatoes into a shallow serving dish. To make the dressing, mix the mayonnaise with the creamed horseradish, lemon juice, double cream or soured cream and salt and pepper to taste, blending well.

Spoon the dressing over the tomatoes to cover partially. Sprinkle with the chives and paprika to serve. Garnish with chives.

SERVES 4

Nutritional content per serving: Carbohydrate: 4 g Fat: 20 g Fibre: 2 g Kilocalories: 206

GERMAN POTATO SALAD

MOST GERMAN POTATO SALADS ARE MADE WITH HOT COOKED POTATOES FINISHED WITH A SPICY DRESSING. THIS ONE ALSO HAS A LITTLE CHOPPED GERMAN SAUSAGE ADDED TO IT. SALAMI, OR ANY SPICY SAUSAGE OF YOUR CHOICE (PERHAPS SOME LEFTOVERS) WOULD MAKE AN EQUALLY GOOD ALTERNATIVE

- 750 g (1½ lb) waxy potatoes, peeled or scrubbed
- ½ bunch spring onions, sliced
- 1 teaspoon capers
- 1 dill pickle, chopped
- 125 g (4 oz) spiced German sausage, diced
- 4 tablespoons Mayonnaise (see page 7)
- 1 tablespoon single cream or natural yogurt
- 1 teaspoon German mustard
- salt and pepper

Cook the potatoes in boiling salted water until tender, about 15-20 minutes, depending upon size. Drain thoroughly, cut into bite-sized pieces and keep warm.

Slice the spring onions, reserving a few whole ones for garnishing and add with the capers, dill pickle and sausage. Mix the mayonnaise with the cream or yogurt, mustard and salt and pepper to taste. Fold into the potato mixture, mixing well to coat.

Serve the salad at once while still warm garnished with the reserved whole spring onions.

SERVES 4-6

Nutritional content per serving: Carbohydrate: 37 g Fat: 21 g Fibre 4 g Kilocalories: 354

YORKSHIRE PLOUGHBOY SALAD

I HAVE NO IDEA WHETHER THERE IS SUCH A THING AS A TYPICAL YORKSHIRE PLOUGHBOY SALAD. ALL I KNOW IS THAT THIS HAS BECOME A FAVOURITE IN MY HOME (AND WAS IN THE HOMES OF MY MOTHER AND GRANDMOTHER BEFORE ME). IT IS A SALAD THAT HAS BEEN PASSED ON FROM GENERATION TO GENERATION, HAS STOOD THE TEST OF TIME AND SO DESERVES THE TITLE OF 'CLASSIC'. IT IS ESPECIALLY DELICIOUS WITH A PLATTER OF COLD ROAST MEATS

- 1 small red cabbage, cored and shredded very finely
- 1 onion, sliced finely
- 1 tablespoon dark treacle or molasses
- 2 tablespoons white wine vinegar
- ½ teaspoon mustard
- salt and pepper
- 4 oz (125 g) Cheddar, Wensleydale, Caerphilly or Cheshire cheese, crumbled or cubed

Place the cabbage in a large bowl with the onion. To make the dressing, mix the treacle or molasses with the vinegar, mustard and salt and pepper to taste. Pour over the cabbage mixture and toss well to coat and mix. Leave to stand for about 15 minutes for the flavours to develop and mature.

Just before serving sprinkle the crumbled or cubed cheese over the salad and toss well.

SERVES 4-6

Nutritional content per serving: Carbohydrate: 10 g Fat: 11 g Fibre: 5 g Kilocalories: 179

Crunchy Coleslaw; Yorkshire Ploughboy Salad; German Potato Salad

CRUNCHY COLESLAW

COLESLAW IS TRADITIONALLY MADE WITH A MAYONNAISE OR CREAMY DRESSING BUT I USE A CLEAR ITALIAN ONE. ALTERNATIVELY, MAKE WITH YOGURT DRESSING (SEE PAGE 93), CREAMY CAPER DRESSING (SEE PAGE 86), OR LOW-CALORIE MAYONNAISE (SEE PAGE 95)

1 medium head white cabbage, cored and shredded finely
4 carrots, grated coarsely
½ onion, chopped finely
50 g (2 oz) raisins (optional)
8 tablespoons Mayonnaise (see page 7)
½ teaspoon caraway or fennel seeds
salt and pepper

Mix the cabbage with the carrots, onion and raisins, if using, in a large serving bowl.

Add the mayonnaise with salt and pepper to taste and toss gently to coat and mix. Sprinkle with the caraway or fennel seeds to serve.

SERVES 6

Nutritional content per serving: Carbohydrate: 13 g Fat: 16 g Fibre: 5 g Kilocalories: 207

Crab Salad

I REMEMBER THAT MY SPECIAL TREAT AS A CHILD, AT THE END OF A SUMMER'S-DAY OUTING TO THE COAST, WAS TO COME HOME LADEN WITH FRESHLY CAUGHT AND COOKED CRABS. WE WOULD SOMETIMES EAT THEM AS A SALAD, SOMETIMES AS A SPREAD. THIS WAS MY MOTHER'S WAY OF SERVING A DRESSED CRAB SALAD. ACCOMPANY WITH TRIANGLES OF WHOLEMEAL OR BROWN BREAD

4 cooked crabs
4 tablespoons Mayonnaise (see page 7)
1 tablespoon single cream
1 tablespoon fresh white breadcrumbs
chilli powder
4 tablespoons lemon juice
1 hard-boiled egg yolk
1 tablespoon chopped parsley
lettuce leaves to serve
1 quantity Basic Mayonnaise (see page 7) or Lemon Mayonnaise (see page 85) to serve
salt

Prepare the crabs as on page 8, extracting the white and brown meat and keeping them separate. Mix the white meat with the mayonnaise. Mix the brown meat with the cream and breadcrumbs. Season both meats with chilli powder, salt and lemon juice to taste.

Wash the crab shells. Pile the white crab meat back into the middle of the shells and arrange the brown meat on either side.

Sieve the hard-boiled egg yolk and arrange it in two stripes down the crab to separate the white meat from the brown. Arrange the parsley alongside in the same way.

Place a little lettuce on each of 4 individual plates or 1 large serving dish and top with the dressed crabs. Serve with additional mayonnaise handed separately.

SERVES 4

Nutritional content per serving: Carbohydrate: 3 g Fat: 19 g Fibre: 1 g Kilocalories: 245

Crab Salad

Lobster Salad

LOBSTER SALAD

4 medium cooked lobsters
about 250 g (8 oz) mixed salad leaves (such as frisée or escarole, lamb's lettuce, watercress, radicchio or batavia lettuce)
4 tablespoons French Dressing (see page 85)
lemon wedges or slices to serve
DRESSING:
1 ripe avocado, peeled and stoned
4 tablespoons soured cream
5 tablespoons natural yogurt
2 tablespoons lemon juice
grated rind of ½ lemon
2 teaspoons chopped tarragon
1 teaspoon snipped chives
salt and pepper

Lay the lobster on its back, detach the legs then insert the pointed end of a sharp knife between the body and tail. Cut down the length of the lobster to the tail, until in half. Halve again. Remove the thread of dark gut, running down the length of the lobster, with the gravel sac at the top of the head, the creamy liver and coral.

Crack the claws with a mallet and remove the flesh. Break the legs apart at the central joint. Remove the flesh with a skewer. Remove the tail flesh and cut into bite-sized pieces. Remove the body meat and flesh attached to the shell.

Place the avocado, cream, yogurt, lemon juice and rind, herbs and salt and pepper to taste in a blender. Purée till smooth.

Mix the lobster with a little of the dressing, or leave plain, and pile back into the shells. Place the salad leaves on 4 individual plates and drizzle with French dressing. Arrange the lobster on top and serve with the lemon and the remaining avocado dressing, handed separately in a jug.

SERVES 4

Nutritional content per serving: Carbohydrate: 3 g Fat: 29 g Fibre: 3 g Kilocalories: 425

BRETON SALAD

THIS FRENCH SALAD WAS DOUBTLESS DEVELOPED TO ACCOMPANY THE PRIZED SALT-MEADOW LAMB AND MUTTON OF INLAND BRITTANY. YOU CAN SUBSTITUTE THE CLASSIC VINAIGRETTE WITH CREAMY CAPER DRESSING (SEE PAGE 86)

375 g (12 oz) fresh haricot beans or 125 g (4 oz) dried beans
250 g (8 oz) cooked beetroot, peeled and sliced
250 g (8 oz) lamb's lettuce or 125 g (4 oz) lamb's lettuce and 125 g (4 oz) watercress
2 tablespoons chopped parsley
6 tablespoons Classic Vinaigrette (see page 85)

Cook the fresh beans in boiling salted water until tender, about 10-15 minutes, depending upon maturity. (If fresh beans are not available then use dried beans. Soak overnight in cold water and cook in fresh water for about 1½-2 hours until tender.)

Drain the cooked beans and mix with the beetroot, lamb's lettuce or lamb's lettuce and watercress, and parsley. Pour over the dressing and toss gently to coat and mix.

Serve at once while the salad is still warm.

SERVES 4

Nutritional content per serving: Carbohydrate: 23 g Fat: 16 g Fibre: 10 g Kilocalories: 259

AMERICAN CREAMY CABBAGE SALAD

PERHAPS AMERICA'S ANSWER TO COLESLAW, THIS CREAMY, CRUNCHY SALAD IS DELICIOUS WITH BARBECUE FARE LIKE JACKET POTATOES, GRILLED STEAKS, HAMBURGERS AND SPARERIBS. FOR A CHANGE, OR TO MAKE A MORE COLOURFUL SALAD, YOU COULD USE RED CABBAGE INSTEAD OF WHITE CABBAGE IN THE COLD WINTER MONTHS

½ small head white cabbage
knob of butter
2 tablespoons single cream
1 egg, separated
1 tablespoon white wine vinegar
salt and pepper
poppy seeds to garnish (optional)

Core and shred the cabbage very finely and place in a large bowl.

Place the butter in a bowl, over a saucepan of hot water, melt, then add the cream and egg yolk, mixing well. Lightly beat the egg white until just stiff and fold into the cream mixture with the vinegar and salt and pepper to taste. Cook until the mixture thickens, stirring constantly, but do not allow to boil. Remove from the heat and allow to cool completely.

When cold, fold into the cabbage mixture and transfer to a serving dish. Sprinkle with poppy seeds before serving, if using.

SERVES 4

Nutritional content per serving: Carbohydrate: 4 g Fat: 3 g Fibre: 2 g Kilocalories: 57

Breton Salad; Spanish Salad; American Creamy Cabbage Salad

Spanish salad

Use only fresh Parmesan cheese for this salad and grate or shave it into paper-thin pieces

1 large Spanish onion
3 extra large tomatoes
¼ cucumber, sliced thinly
about 8 pimiento-stuffed olives, sliced
about 4 tablespoons grated or shaved fresh Parmesan cheese
4 tablespoons French Dressing (see page 85)
salt and pepper

Thinly slice the onion and tomatoes and layer on individual shallow serving dishes with the cucumber, olives and Parmesan cheese.

Just before serving, sprinkle with salt and pepper to taste and drizzle over the dressing. Serve at once.

SERVES 4-6

Nutritional content per serving: Carbohydrate: 8 g Fat: 17 g Fibre: 4 g Kilocalories: 213

Flemish salad

This salad uses salted or pickled herrings, for which the Dutch have a particular passion. It makes a delicious lunch dish, served with plenty of rye bread

- 1 large waxy potato, boiled and diced
- 175 g (6 oz) cooked beetroot, diced
- 2 small green dessert apples, cored and chopped
- 1 large dill pickle, chopped
- ½ mild Spanish or 1 red onion, sliced
- 2 salted or pickled herrings
- 6 tablespoons Mayonnaise (see page 7)
- 1 hard-boiled egg, sliced
- salt and pepper
- 1 tablespoon snipped chives or parsley to garnish

Mix the potato with the beetroot, apple, dill pickle and onion rings. Flake the fish or cut into small pieces and add to the potato mixture.

Add the mayonnaise with salt and pepper to taste and toss very gently to coat and mix. Spoon into a shallow serving bowl and top with the egg slices. Sprinkle with chives or parsley and serve as soon as possible.

SERVES 4

Nutritional content per serving: Carbohydrate: 23 g Fat: 28 g Fibre: 4 g Kilocalories: 390

TABBOULEH

CLASSIC TABBOULEH IS BASED ON BULGAR WHEAT, MINT, SPRING ONIONS AND CUCUMBER IN A DRESSING. HOWEVER, I SOMETIMES LIKE TO ADD A LITTLE CHOPPED RED PEPPER AND TOMATO TO MAKE THIS SALAD MORE COLOURFUL

75 g (3 oz) bulgar wheat
3 tablespoons chopped mint
5 tablespoons chopped parsley
4 spring onions, chopped finely
½ cucumber, chopped finely
3 tablespoons lemon juice
2 tablespoons olive oil
2 tomatoes, skinned, deseeded and chopped (optional)
¼ red pepper, cored, deseeded and chopped finely (optional)
salt and pepper
mint sprigs to garnish

Place the bulgar wheat in a bowl with cold water to cover. Leave to soak for 1 hour, then drain and squeeze out as much moisture as possible from the grains. This is best done in a muslin cloth. Place in a bowl with the mint, parsley, spring onions and cucumber.

Beat the lemon juice with the oil and salt and pepper to taste until well blended. Fold into the wheat mixture with the tomatoes and red pepper, if used, to coat and mix. Spoon into a shallow serving dish to serve. Garnish with mint sprigs.

SERVES 4

Nutritional content per serving: Carbohydrate: 14 g Fat: 8 g Fibre: 2 g Kilocalories: 140

GAZPACHO SALAD

SERVE THIS CLASSIC TOMATO, PEPPER, CUCUMBER AND ONION SALAD WITH A SELECTION OF ACCOMPANIMENTS, JUST AS YOU WOULD PRESENT CHILLED GAZPACHO SOUP – GARLIC CROÛTONS (SEE PAGE 95) AND CHOPPED HARD-BOILED EGGS, FOR EXAMPLE, WOULD BOTH COMPLEMENT THE FLAVOUR OF THIS FRESH SALAD. ALTERNATIVELY SERVE IT WITH CHUNKS OF PIPING HOT GARLIC BREAD

6 tomatoes, diced
2 green peppers, cored, deseeded and sliced
½ cucumber, chopped or sliced finely
1 onion, chopped or sliced into rings
2 tablespoons chopped mixed herbs (for example, parsley, chervil, chives, basil and tarragon)
6 tablespoons Classic Vinaigrette (see page 85)
pinch of ground cumin
1 shallot or small red onion, chopped very finely
salt and pepper

Place the layers of the tomatoes, peppers, cucumber and onion in a salad bowl, sprinkling between each layer with salt and pepper and half of the herbs.

Just before serving, mix the vinaigrette with the cumin, shallot or onion and remaining herbs and pour over the salad. Either toss to serve or serve still arranged in layers.

SERVES 4

Nutritional content per serving: Carbohydrate: 6 g Fat: 15 g Fibre: 3 g Kilocalories: 168

Tabbouleh; Flemish Salad; Gazpacho Salad

Italian Pepper Salad

The coloured peppers in this recipe can be grilled, skin-side upwards and the skins removed before cooking with the other ingredients, to give a softer texture and slightly milder flavour

500 g (1 lb) mixed coloured peppers (such as red, yellow, green, black and white)
8 small black olives
2 teaspoons chopped mixed herbs
1 teaspoon tomato purée
3 tablespoons olive oil
2 tablespoons red wine vinegar
1 onion, sliced
salt and pepper

Core, deseed and slice the peppers and place in a pan with the olives, herbs, tomato purée, oil, vinegar, onion and salt and pepper to taste. Mix well, cover with a tight-fitting lid and bring to the boil. Reduce the heat and simmer, covered, for 15-20 minutes or until the peppers are just soft. Remove from the heat and allow to cool.

Chill thoroughly and mix well just before serving.

SERVES 4-6

Nutritional content per serving: Carbohydrate: 4 g Fat: 13 g Fibre: 2 g Kilocalories: 135

Sauerkraut and Smoked Fish Salad

This is a classic German sauerkraut salad, the flavour of which can be varied slightly by introducing different herbs and spices. Serve with a variety of breads, warmed and cut into chunks

500 g (1 lb) canned or bottled sauerkraut, rinsed and drained
2 sticks celery, chopped
½ red pepper, cored, deseeded and chopped
2 tablespoons hazelnuts, halved
1 tart apple, cored and sliced
500 g (1 lb) smoked fish, sliced thinly into bite-sized pieces
6 tablespoons Citrus Vinaigrette (see Classic Vinaigrette, page 85)
salt and pepper

Place the sauerkraut in a bowl and separate with the fingers or with two forks. Add the celery, red pepper, hazelnuts, apple and fish. Toss gently to mix.

Pour the dressing over the salad just before serving, add salt and pepper to taste and toss gently to coat and mix.

Variation: A pinch of ground cloves will give this salad a spicy flavour, and a little chilli pepper will make it hotter. Alternatively try adding ½ teaspoon caraway seeds or 1 teaspoon finely grated fresh root ginger when you mix in the celery, pepper, nuts, apple and fish.

SERVES 4

Nutritional content per serving: Carbohydrate: 6 g Fat: 18 g Fibre: 5 g Kilocalories: 289

Swiss Salad; Italian Pepper Salad; Sauerkraut and Smoked Fish Salad

Swiss salad

Serve this side salad with other cold mixed salads as part of a cold buffet spread. Alternatively, double the quantities given here and serve it as a light lunch or supper dish

- 250 g (8 oz) cooked potatoes, diced
- 2 cooked carrots, diced
- 1 tart apple, cored and chopped
- 1 cooked herring, skinned, boned and flaked
- 2 tablespoons chopped parsley
- 4 tablespoons Mint Dressing (see page 87)
- salt and pepper

Mix the potatoes with the carrots, apple, herring and parsley. Pour over the dressing with salt and pepper to taste and toss gently to coat and mix.

Transfer to a shallow serving dish and chill the salad thoroughly before serving.

SERVES 4

Nutritional content per serving: Carbohydrate: 17 g Fat: 14 g Fibre: 3 g Kilocalories: 225

Jamaican Lemon Pickle Salad

Serve this spicy orange and green salad mixture with plain roast meats, or barbecued meats, poultry or fish

- about 250 g (8 oz) lamb's lettuce
- 1 bunch watercress
- 2 tablespoons sunflower seeds (optional)
- 1 teaspoon tarragon leaves
- 4 ordinary or blood oranges
- grated rind of 1 orange
- pinch of chilli powder
- 6 tablespoons French Dressing (see page 85) or Honey Dressing (see page 86)
- 1 tablespoon chopped lemon pickle
- salt

Separate the lamb's lettuce into leaves, wash, dry, then place in a serving bowl. Add the watercress, sunflower seeds, if used, and tarragon.

Remove the peel and pith from the oranges and cut the flesh into very thin slices or segments. Sprinkle with the orange rind, chilli powder and a little salt to taste. Add to the salad leaf mixture.

Mix the chosen dressing with the lemon pickle. Pour over the salad and toss gently to coat and mix. Serve at once.

SERVES 4

Nutritional content per serving: Carbohydrate: 3 g Fat: 27 g Fibre: 6 g Kilocalories: 272

Jamaican Lemon Pickle Salad

Italian Fennel Salad

ITALIAN FENNEL SALAD

FENNEL, A FIST-SIZED WHITE BULB WITH RIBBED LEAVES AND PALE GREEN FRONDS, HAS A HIGHLY AROMATIC, FRESH ANISEED FLAVOUR THAT THE ITALIANS ADORE. HERE IT IS COMBINED WITH TWO OF THEIR OTHER GREAT LOVES, SEAFOOD AND MINT

2 bulbs fennel
¼ cucumber, chopped finely
6 radishes, sliced finely
175 g (6 oz) cooked mussels, shrimps or flaked crab
1 small red dessert apple, peeled, cored and sliced
DRESSING:
4 tablespoons olive oil
1 egg yolk
2 teaspoons chopped mint
2 teaspoons red wine vinegar
salt and pepper

Trim the fennel, reserving the fronds, then cut into slices. Place in a bowl with the cucumber, radishes, shellfish and apple.

To make the dressing, beat the oil with the egg yolk, mint, vinegar and salt and pepper to taste until well blended. Pour over the salad and toss gently to coat and mix.

Garnish with the reserved fennel fronds before serving.

SERVES 4

Nutritional content per serving: Carbohydrate: 7 g Fat: 18 g Fibre: 4 g Kilocalories: 245

TZATZIKI SALAD

THIS COOL, REFRESHING GREEK SALAD MUST BE MADE WITH THICK GREEK OR THICK SET NATURAL YOGURT – ORDINARY YOGURT SEEMS TOO WATERY. SERVE WITH GRILLED KEBABS AND OTHER BARBECUE FARE, OR AS A STARTER WITH FINGERS OF WARM PITTA BREAD

- 1 large cucumber
- 2 tablespoons chopped mint
- 4 teaspoons chopped parsley
- 450 g (14 oz) carton Greek yogurt
- 2 cloves garlic, crushed
- ½ teaspoon paprika
- salt
- mint sprigs to garnish

Cut the cucumber into small dice or grate it coarsely. Place in a bowl and add the mint and parsley, blending well.

Mix the yogurt with the garlic, salt to taste and half of the paprika. Fold into the cucumber mixture to blend and coat. Spoon into a shallow serving dish, sprinkle with the remaining paprika and garnish with mint sprigs.

Serve lightly chilled.

SERVES 6

Nutritional content per serving: Carbohydrate: 11 g Fat: 3 g Fibre: 1 g Kilocalories: 99

RUSSIAN SALAD

THIS SALAD IS BEST MADE WHEN YOUNG SPRING PEAS, CARROTS AND BEANS ARE IN SEASON. HOWEVER, IT IS ALSO WORTH REMEMBERING WHEN THESE VEGETABLES AND A LITTLE ROAST OR COOKED MEAT ARE LEFT OVER FROM ANOTHER MEAL

- 3 large cooked potatoes, diced
- 125 g (4 oz) cooked peas
- 125 g (4 oz) cooked green beans, halved if large
- 4 medium or 6 small cooked carrots, diced
- ½ onion, chopped finely
- 125 g (4 oz) cooked chicken, skinned and chopped
- 50 g (2 oz) cooked tongue, chopped
- 50 g (2 oz) garlic sausage or salami, chopped
- ¾ quantity Mayonnaise (see page 7)
- 2 tablespoons snipped chives
- 1 tablespoon chopped parsley
- pinch of chilli powder
- 2 hard-boiled eggs

Place the potatoes, peas, beans, carrots, onion, chicken, tongue and garlic sausage or salami in a large mixing bowl and toss gently to mix.

Blend the mayonnaise with half of the chives, the parsley and chilli powder. Add to the salad mixture and toss gently to coat and mix. Spoon into a serving bowl.

Shell the eggs and cut into wedges. Arrange on the Russian salad mixture and sprinkle the eggs with the remaining chives. Cover and chill thoroughly before serving.

SERVES 4-6

Nutritional content per serving: Carbohydrate: 31 g Fat: 76 g Fibre: 9 g Kilocalories: 898

Tzatziki Salad; Salad Elona; Russian Salad

SALAD ELONA

THE PERFECT SUMMER DISH, SALAD ELONA IS A SIMPLE COMBINATION OF CUCUMBER AND SLICED STRAWBERRIES. FOR SPECIAL OCCASIONS MAKE IT WITH WILD STRAWBERRIES (*FRAISES DU BOIS* OR ALPINE STRAWBERRIES). THEY ARE SMALLER BUT MORE AROMATIC THAN THE ORDINARY CULTIVATED VARIETY AND MAKE THIS DISH A REAL TREAT

- 1 small cucumber, peeled and sliced very thinly
- 1 punnet (or about 12 medium) strawberries, sliced
- 2 tablespoons dry white wine
- ½ teaspoon white wine vinegar
- salt and pepper
- dill sprigs to garnish

Arrange the cucumber and strawberry slices attractively on a large serving plate.

Mix the wine with the wine vinegar and salt and pepper to taste. Spoon over the salad, cover and chill for at least 30 minutes.

Serve lightly chilled, garnished with dill sprigs.

SERVES 4

Nutritional content per serving: Carbohydrate: 4 g Fibre: 1 g Kilocalories: 24

SALAD DRESSINGS

RICH, SMOOTH AND CREAMY; SHARP, CLEAR AND FRUITY; OR PIQUANT, AROMATIC AND VIRTUALLY CALORIE-FREE, THERE IS A DRESSING FOR EVERY SALAD TYPE. FOR THE BEST RESULTS ADD TO A SALAD JUST BEFORE SERVING SO THAT FLAVOURS ARE STILL FRESH AND DISTINCTIVE.

HERB MAYONNAISE

2 egg yolks or 1 egg
1 tablespoon white wine vinegar
½ teaspoon salt
½ teaspoon dry mustard powder
pinch of freshly ground white pepper
300 ml (½ pint) olive oil (at room temperature)
2 tablespoons chopped mixed herbs (for example, parsley, chives, tarragon, chervil, rosemary and thyme)

Beat the egg yolks or egg with the vinegar, salt, mustard and pepper to make a smooth paste. Slowly beat in the oil, drop by drop to begin with, beating well until thickened. Gradually add the remaining oil in a steady stream, beating until smooth and thick.

Alternatively, place the paste in an electric blender or food processor and gradually add the oil, with the blender set on a low speed or the food processor set on medium speed, until it has all been incorporated and the dressing is thick and creamy.

Adjust the seasoning if necessary and add the herbs.

Variations

Curry Mayonnaise: Add 1-2 teaspoons curry powder and 1 teaspoon mango chutney to the prepared mayonnaise, stirring well to blend.
Lemon Mayonnaise: Use the lemon juice rather than the vinegar and add 1 teaspoon finely grated lemon rind to the prepared mayonnaise.

MAKES 300 ML (½ PINT)

Nutritional content per quantity: Fat: 318 g Fibre: 2 g Kilocalories: 2905

CLASSIC VINAIGRETTE

175 ml (6 fl oz) olive oil
4 tablespoons white wine vinegar, cider vinegar or tarragon vinegar
1 teaspoon clear honey
2 tablespoons chopped mixed herbs
1 clove garlic, crushed
salt and pepper

Beat the oil with the chosen vinegar, honey, herbs, garlic and salt and pepper to taste until well blended. Alternatively, place all the ingredients in a screw-top jar and shake vigorously to blend before using.

Variation: To make a Citrus Vinaigrette, simply substitute fresh lemon, lime or grapefruit juice for the vinegar in the recipe above.

MAKES ABOUT 250 ML (8 FL OZ)

Nutritional content per quantity: Carbohydrate: 5 g Fat: 175 g Fibre: 1 g Kilocalories: 1598

FRENCH DRESSING

200 ml (7 fl oz) olive oil
5 tablespoons white wine vinegar
½ teaspoon wholegrain mustard
1 clove garlic, crushed
small strip of lemon rind
few whole sprigs of herbs
salt and pepper

Place the oil, vinegar, mustard, garlic, lemon rind, herbs and salt and pepper to taste in a large screw-top jar or bottle. Shake vigorously to blend before using.

MAKES ABOUT 300 ML (½ PINT)

Nutritional content per quantity: Carbohydrate: 2 g Fat: 200 g Kilocalories: 1813

Herb Mayonnaise; Classic Vinaigrette; French Dressing

Honey dressing

This light and refreshing dressing can also be made with herbs. Simply add 1 tablespoon chopped mixed or single-variety herbs to the dressing and mix well to blend. The type of honey you use will also vary the flavour – experiment with orange blossom (citrus-tasting), acacia (mild and runny) and Jamaican (dark, with a hint of tropical flowers)

- 2 tablespoons clear honey
- 4 tablespoons lemon juice
- 3 tablespoons olive or sunflower oil
- salt and pepper

Beat the honey with the lemon juice, oil and salt and pepper to taste until well blended. Alternatively, place all the ingredients in a screw-top jar or bottle and shake vigorously to blend before using.

MAKES ABOUT 150 ML (¼ PINT)

Nutritional content per quantity: Carbohydrate: 24 g Fat: 45 g Kilocalories: 495

Creamy caper dressing

This is a recipe for a rich, creamy and piquant caper dressing that is ideal to serve with lamb or fish salads

- 2 tablespoons olive oil
- 1½ teaspoons white wine vinegar
- 3 hard-boiled egg yolks
- 2 teaspoons Dijon mustard
- ½ clove garlic, crushed
- 2 tablespoons lemon juice
- 1 teaspoon chopped dill
- 2 teaspoons chopped capers
- salt and pepper

Beat the oil with the vinegar. Mash the hard-boiled egg yolks until smooth then gradually add the oil mixture, beating well until smooth.

Gradually add the mustard, garlic and lemon juice and mix to a creamy dressing. Fold in the dill, capers and salt and pepper to taste. Serve lightly chilled.

MAKES ABOUT 125 ML (4 FL OZ)

Nutritional content per quantity: Carbohydrate: 3 g Fat: 59 g Kilocalories: 600

Blue cheese dressing

Light and creamy yet sharp, this dressing goes well with pasta, potato or crisp lettuce salads. Alternatively, spoon into scooped-out halves of fresh dessert pears and serve as a starter

- 150 ml (5 fl oz) carton soured cream
- 75 g (3 oz) blue cheese
- 2 teaspoons chopped mixed herbs (for example, chives, tarragon, parsley and basil)
- 1 tablespoon lemon juice

Place the soured cream and blue cheese in a blender or food processor and purée until smooth. Add the herbs and lemon juice and mix well. Spoon into a serving dish, cover and leave to stand for at least 30 minutes for the flavours to combine and develop.

MAKES ABOUT 200 ML (7 FL OZ)

Nutritional content per quantity: Carbohydrate: 4 g Fat: 74 g Fibre: 0.5 g Kilocalories: 766

Creamy Caper Dressing; Honey Dressing; Mint Dressing; Blue Cheese Dressing

MINT DRESSING

6 tablespoons olive oil
2 tablespoons lemon juice
2–3 tablespoons chopped mint
pinch of sugar
salt and pepper

Beat the oil with the lemon juice, mint, sugar and salt and pepper to taste until well blended. Alternatively, place all the ingredients in a screw-top jar and shake vigorously to blend.

Leave to stand for at least 15 minutes for the flavours to develop, then beat or shake again before using.

MAKES ABOUT 125 ML (4 FL OZ)

Nutritional content per quantity: Carbohydrate: 7 g Fat: 90 g Fibre: 0.5 g Kilocalories: 840

Soured cream and orange dressing

This is a delicious creamy dressing to serve with a green salad or even to top a fruit salad

250 ml (8 fl oz) soured cream
grated rind and juice of 1 orange
2 tablespoons lemon juice
1 teaspoon caster sugar
salt and pepper

Mix the soured cream with the orange rind and juice, lemon juice and caster sugar. Season to taste with salt and pepper. Chill lightly then stir well before serving.

MAKES ABOUT 300 ML (½ PINT)

Nutritional content per quantity: Carbohydrate: 23 g Fat: 45 g Fibre: 3 g Kilocalories: 517

THOUSAND ISLAND DRESSING

THIS CLASSIC, COLOURFUL AND CREAMY DRESSING HAS MANY VARIATIONS – THIS IS MY FAVOURITE. SHOULD YOU WISH TO MAKE IT LIGHTER, THEN SUBSTITUTE THICK SET NATURAL YOGURT FOR HALF OF THE MAYONNAISE. MARY ROSE DRESSING, A FAVOURITE WITH SHELLFISH, CAN ALSO BE MADE FOLLOWING THE RECIPE BELOW (SEE VARIATION)

½ quantity Mayonnaise (see page 7)
½ teaspoon paprika
1 teaspoon minced onion
pinch of garlic salt
½ teaspoon tomato purée
2 teaspoons chopped parsley
40 g (1½ oz) red pepper, chopped finely
40 g (1½ oz) green pepper, chopped finely
40 g (1½ oz) celery, chopped finely
2 green olives or 1 small gherkin, chopped finely

Mix the mayonnaise with the paprika, onion, garlic salt and tomato purée in a bowl. Add the parsley, peppers, celery and olives or gherkin and mix well to blend. Leave to stand for at least 15 minutes for the flavours to develop before using.

Variation: To make Mary Rose dressing, suitable for serving with shellfish salads, omit the chopped parsley, peppers, celery and olives.

MAKES ABOUT 200 ML (7 FL OZ)

Nutritional content per quantity: Carbohydrate: 4 g Fat: 162 g Fibre: 3 g Kilocalories: 1501

RASPBERRY DRESSING

YOU COULD ALSO MAKE THIS FRUITY SALAD DRESSING WITH STRAWBERRY VINEGAR OR, SHOULD YOU BE SO FORTUNATE, CHAMPAGNE VINEGAR. THE USE OF TWO OILS MAKES THE DRESSING ALL THE MORE INTERESTING. IT IS DELICIOUS WITH GREEN SALADS AND SALADS MADE WITH MILD VEGETABLES, SUCH AS COURGETTES

3 tablespoons sunflower oil
2 tablespoons sesame oil
3 tablespoons raspberry vinegar
salt and pepper

Beat the oils with the vinegar and salt and pepper to taste until well blended. Alternatively, place all the ingredients in a screw-top jar or bottle and shake vigorously to blend before using.

Variation: Home-made fruit vinegars, based on any of the soft berries that will macerate, can be used in the recipe to create a range of fruity dressings.

For a herb flavour, replace the fruit vinegar with a good herb wine vinegar which has tarragon, rosemary or thyme in it.

MAKES 125 ML (4 FL OZ)

Nutritional content per quantity: Fat: 75 g Kilocalories: 676

Raspberry Dressing; Soured Cream and Orange Dressing; Thousand Island Dressing

SHERRIED DRESSING

THIS RICH, CREAMY AND DISTINCTIVE DRESSING IS PERFECT TO SERVE WITH ANY FRUIT-BASED SALAD OR A PLAIN LEAF SALAD ASSORTMENT WHICH INCLUDES FRISÉE OR RADICCHIO

1 egg
2 tablespoons dry sherry
2 tablespoons sugar
1 tablespoon melted butter
juice of 1 orange
2 tablespoons lemon juice
4 tablespoons double cream
salt and pepper
chopped parsley (optional)

Beat the egg with the sherry, sugar, butter, orange juice, lemon juice and salt and pepper to taste.

Place in a small saucepan and cook over a low heat, whisking constantly, until the mixture thickens, but do not bring it to the boil. Allow to cool completely.

Whip the cream until it stands in soft peaks and fold into the cool dressing. Spoon into a serving bowl and sprinkle with chopped parsley if using.

MAKES ABOUT 200 ML (7 FL OZ)

Nutritional content per quantity: Carbohydrate: 41 g Fat: 48 g Kilocalories: 651

TOMATO JUICE DRESSING

IT IS A SURE SIGN THAT I AM WATCHING MY WEIGHT AGAIN WHEN THIS DRESSING GAINS PRIDE OF PLACE IN THE DOOR OF MY REFRIGERATOR. IT IS A GOOD, VERSATILE DRESSING THAT REALLY DOES CUT DOWN ON THE CALORIES OF CONVENTIONAL DRESSINGS AS IT INCLUDES NO OIL. THIS DRESSING WILL KEEP FOR 3-4 DAYS IN THE REFRIGERATOR

300 ml (½ pint) tomato juice
1–2 cloves garlic, crushed
dash of Tabasco sauce
25 g (1 oz) onion, chopped finely
1 tablespoon chopped mixed herbs (for example, parsley, tarragon, chives, basil and chervil)
salt and pepper

Mix the tomato juice with the garlic, Tabasco sauce, onion, herbs and salt and pepper to taste until well blended.

Alternatively, place all the ingredients in a screw-top jar or bottle and shake vigorously to blend.

Ideally leave for at least 2-3 hours before using to allow the flavours to mature.

Variation: Make this dressing more spicy by adding a sprinkling of paprika or chilli powder. You could also include chopped green pepper, gherkins and cucumber to give it more body.

MAKES ABOUT 300 ML (½ PINT)

Nutritional content per quantity: Carbohydrate: 13 g Fibre: 1 g Kilocalories: 61

Tomato Juice Dressing; Normandy Dressing; Sherried Dressing

NORMANDY DRESSING

THIS SIMPLE BUT SUMPTUOUS CREAMY DRESSING IS SPLENDID DRIZZLED OVER LIGHT, CRISP, SPRING AND SUMMER SALADS MADE WITH A SELECTION OF YOUNG, LEAFY VEGETABLES

2 tablespoons lemon juice
4 tablespoons extra thick double cream
½ teaspoon finely grated lemon rind
1 tablespoon snipped chives
salt and pepper

Place the lemon juice, cream, lemon rind, chives and salt and pepper to taste in a bowl and whisk until well blended and creamy. Cover and chill until required.

MAKES ABOUT 100 ML (3½ FL OZ)

Nutritional content per quantity: Carbohydrate: 2 g Fat: 29 g Fibre: 1 g Kilocalories: 272

CHIFFONADE DRESSING

A GOOD, ALL-ROUND DRESSING WITH A COLOURFUL APPEARANCE. CHILL THOROUGHLY AND SERVE VERY COLD

2 hard-boiled eggs
¼ small red pepper, cored, deseeded and chopped very finely
2 tablespoons chopped parsley
½ small shallot or spring onion, chopped very finely
½ quantity French Dressing (see page 85)

Shell the eggs and chop very finely or press through a fine sieve. Add the red pepper, parsley and shallot, mixing well. Gradually add the French dressing and mix to a smooth consistency. Cover and chill thoroughly until required.

If this dressing seems a little too thick for tossing rather than coating purposes, then add a little more French dressing to thin.

MAKES ABOUT 200 ML (7 FL OZ)

Nutritional content per quantity: Carbohydrate: 4 g Fat: 113 g Fibre: 1 g Kilocalories: 1120

PORT DRESSING

THE PERFECT FESTIVE SEASON DRESSING FOR CRISP LETTUCE OR MELON SALADS. IF AVAILABLE, A LITTLE CHOPPED TARRAGON CAN BE ADDED JUST BEFORE SERVING TO INTRODUCE A SUBTLE HERBY FLAVOUR

6 tablespoons sunflower oil
3 tablespoons red wine vinegar
100 ml (3½ fl oz) port
1 teaspoon chopped tarragon (optional)
salt and pepper

Beat the oil with the vinegar, port and salt and pepper to taste until well blended. Alternatively, place all the ingredients in a screw-top jar or bottle and shake vigorously to blend.

Add the tarragon, if used, just before serving, mixing or shaking well to combine.

MAKES ABOUT 250 ML (8 FL OZ)

Nutritional content per quantity: Carbohydrate: 12 g Fat: 90 g Kilocalories: 968

SPICED ORANGE MAYONNAISE

A WARM, SUBTLE, YET FRESH-TASTING MAYONNAISE DRESSING THAT IS PERFECT TO SERVE WITH ANY DUCK, GAME AND RICH MEAT SALADS MADE WITH A SELECTION OF CITRUS FRUITS

8 tablespoons Mayonnaise (see page 7)
finely grated rind of 1 orange
4 teaspoons tomato purée
2 teaspoons mild curry powder
1 teaspoon English mustard
2 tablespoons single cream
salt and pepper

Mix the mayonnaise with the orange rind, tomato purée, curry powder, mustard and cream, blending well. Season to taste with salt and pepper. Cover and leave to stand for at least 15 minutes for the flavours to develop.

MAKES ABOUT 150 ML (¼ PINT)

Nutritional content per quantity: Carbohydrate: 3 g Fat: 122 g Kilocalories: 1131

Spiced Orange Mayonnaise; Port Dressing; Yogurt Dressing; Chiffonade Dressing

YOGURT DRESSING

THIS IS A VERSATILE, LOW-CALORIE SALAD DRESSING THAT CAN BE VARIED BY ADDING CHOPPED MIXED HERBS, GRATED CITRUS ZEST, A LITTLE CURRY PASTE, CHOPPED PICKLES, CRUSHED GARLIC OR TOMATO PURÉE

- 150 g (5.3 oz carton) thick set natural yogurt
- 1 tablespoon lemon juice
- 1 teaspoon clear honey
- ¼ teaspoon mustard
- salt and pepper

Beat the yogurt with the lemon juice, honey, mustard and salt and pepper to taste until smooth and creamy. Serve lightly chilled.

MAKES ABOUT 150 ML (¼ PINT)

Nutritional content per quantity: Carbohydrate: 15 g Fat: 5 g Kilocalories: 130

CHEESY LEMON DRESSING

USE THIS DELICIOUSLY SMOOTH AND CREAMY DRESSING AS AN ALTERNATIVE TO MAYONNAISE – IT IS ESPECIALLY GOOD WITH FISH SALADS

125 g (4 oz) full-fat soft cheese
4 tablespoons sunflower oil
2 tablespoons lemon juice
1 teaspoon grated lemon rind
½ teaspoon mild mustard
salt and pepper

Beat the cheese until softened, then gradually add the oil, lemon juice and lemon rind and mix until smooth and creamy. Season with the mustard and salt and pepper to taste. Serve lightly chilled.

MAKES ABOUT 150 ML (¼ PINT)

Nutritional content per quantity: Carbohydrate: 1 g Fat: 119 g Kilocalories: 1095

Roquefort and Chive Dressing; Cheesy Lemon Dressing; Low-Calorie Mayonnaise; Croûtons

ROQUEFORT AND CHIVE DRESSING

ROQUEFORT IS A DISTINCTIVE BLUE CHEESE WITH A RICH, STRONG AND SALTY FLAVOUR; IT WILL PROBABLY MAKE THIS SALAD DRESSING SUFFICIENTLY SALTY FOR MOST PALATES, SO DO NOT ADD ANY EXTRA SALT UNTIL YOU HAVE THOROUGHLY INCORPORATED THE CHEESE AND TASTED THE RESULTS. SERVE WITH CRISP GREEN SALADS AND POTATO SALADS

175 ml (6 fl oz) olive oil
4 tablespoons sherry vinegar or white wine vinegar
50 g (2 oz) Roquefort cheese, crumbled
2 tablespoons snipped chives
salt and pepper

Beat the oil with the vinegar until well blended. Place the cheese in a bowl and mash until creamy. Gradually add the oil and vinegar mixture, beating well to make a smooth creamy dressing. Fold in the snipped chives.

Taste the dressing and add salt and pepper to taste, if necessary. Cover and chill until required.

MAKES ABOUT 250 ML (8 FL OZ)

Nutritional content per quantity: Fat: 189 g Fibre: 0.5 g Kilocalories: 1754

LOW-CALORIE MAYONNAISE

I FIND THAT THE SPEEDIEST WAY OF MAKING A LOW-CALORIE MAYONNAISE IS TO REPLACE HALF OF A NORMAL QUANTITY OF MAYONNAISE WITH LOW-FAT THICK SET NATURAL YOGURT. HOWEVER, WHEN YOU HAVE A LITTLE MORE TIME TRY THE RECIPE BELOW

2 hard-boiled egg yolks
1 tablespoon white wine vinegar
1 tablespoon lemon or lime juice
pinch of dried mustard powder
pinch or few drops of artificial sweetener (optional)
2 tablespoons low-fat natural yogurt
salt and pepper

Mash the egg yolks with the vinegar, lemon or lime juice, mustard powder and salt and pepper to taste. Add the sweetener if used and mix well.

Beat the yogurt into the seasoned mixture to blend. Cover and leave to stand for 5-10 minutes to allow the flavours to develop.

MAKES ABOUT 100 ML (3½ FL OZ)

Nutritional content per quantity: Carbohydrate: 3 g Fat: 19 g Kilocalories: 234

CROÛTONS

1 large slice day old bread
½ oz (15 g) butter
2 tablespoons vegetable oil

Trim the crust from the slice of bread and cut into even-sized cubes, stars, hearts or circles, using small pastry cutters.

Heat the butter and oil in a frying pan until very hot, add the bread cubes or shapes and fry until crisp and golden brown. Remove with a slotted spoon and drain on kitchen paper. Use while still warm or allow to cool. Add to a salad just before serving.

Variation: To make garlic croûtons prepare as above but fry 1 large garlic clove in the butter and oil mixture for 3 minutes, remove before adding the bread cubes or shapes and fry as above.

MAKES APPROXIMATELY 20 CROÛTONS

Nutritional content per quantity: Carbohydrate: 15 g Fat: 43 g Fibre: 1 g Kilocalories: 451

INDEX